PRAISE FOR *WHERE ...*

A missionary calling leads a Baptist family on a fateful journey to China, leaving a lasting legacy

Twelve years ago, in a board meeting of International Ministries, I first heard the powerful story of a young survivor who had lost his American missionary parents in a plane crash in rural China. I never imagined how fully that story would come alive—covered in real flesh and tears—when I committed to travel with the author to help him fill in the missing details and learn about his parents and that awful crash through hearing the recollections of direct and indirect witnesses. I still remember the powerful sense of God's presence as we stood in the field where the plane crash had occurred.

"Paul, we will leave the video camera on but we will give you a moment alone to talk to your family." I stood at a distance and prayed that that moment would bring the author closure—or more than closure—a sense of reunion with his family.

Where the Cotton Grows is more than a moving story; it is an invitation to each of us to revisit our own lives and family journeys. Perhaps through our reading and reflection, we too will uncover new understandings of our own past that will reshape our future.

—Rev. Dr. Benjamin Shun Lai Chan
Area Director of East and South Asia
International Ministries of American Baptist Churches USA

On January 28, 1947, a plane carrying twenty-seven adults and children, twelve of whom were American and Canadian missionaries, crashed ninety miles west of Hankow, China, killing all on board except one small child, the author of this book. Paul Vick was 16 months old when his parents and his three-year-old brother lost their lives on the Vicks' inaugural missionary journey. The story that Paul narrates here is one of deep faith, clear vision, unwavering courage, parental love, and the divine-human connection that prompts people to care for complete strangers.

I found this book to be a riveting read, captivating me with its vivid detail and unfolding human drama. At various times I found myself scanning a map of China, researching older aircraft, living vicariously through the characters, and being deeply moved by the human pathos of love, loss, rescue, and remembrance. This is a must-read for every person who loves God's mission in the world. But for all people, this is a remarkable story of how God works in seemingly ordinary lives.

This is not just the story of lives lost. More importantly, this is the story of a life's worth. You might assume that missionaries whose lives ended at the very beginning of their service were somehow lost to the economy of God. But in fact Robert and Dorothy Vick touched many lives prior to their call to mission service, during their days of preparation for overseas work, and indeed even as they made their way to that fateful flight. All of this fulfilled God's great purposes in profound ways, not the least of which was the ministry that would one day spring to life in their surviving son, Paul.

I encourage everyone who believes God has a plan for his or her life, and everyone who wonders if God has a plan for his or her life, to read this book.

—**Reginald Mills, MDiv., PhD**
Past President of the Board of Directors of American Baptist
International Ministries

Throughout this deeply personal narrative that is so much more than a memoir, the son of commissioned American Baptist missionaries graces us with glimpses of love, family, faith, strength, and resilience that shaped his sense of personhood. Nurtured and raised by loving grandparents, aunts, and uncles, the author's travels always bring him back to Rochester, New York. In *Where the Cotton Grows*, Paul Vick comes home to himself and, like his parents, prays that his life will continue to bear fruit in his service to church and world.

—**Rev. Angela Sims, PhD**
President of Colgate Rochester Crozer Divinity School

Paul Vick has produced a riveting story of the Vick family legacy that has molded and been molded by the American Baptist Churches of the USA. Beginning with the story of the tragic demise of his parents and brother in a Chinese cotton field in 1947, the surviving orphan scribes a history of American Baptist education, missions, churchmanship, leadership, and ministry that can only be matched by a small number of family units. Paul's writing is tight, leaving out extraneous information that can detract from the story of this iconic, middle-class family that was faithful to the local church and its global mission.

We are given a model of how local congregations can impact one family and how that one family can then impact the world. Paul Vick gives us hope for Christian family life, local church loyalty, denominational effectiveness, and world-wide engagement.

The warm-hearted feel of this publication will affirm the 1846 prayer of Adoniram Judson for the Gardner Colby family in Boston: "May they, and their children, and their children's children, in every generation to the end of time, follow each other in uninterrupted succession through the gates of glory." I strongly recommend *Where the Cotton Grows* for an uplifting perspective on the quiet leaven of a family that makes church involvement a high priority.

—**Jerry B. Cain**
Chancellor, Judson University

I grew up hearing the Vick name and knowing the broad brushstrokes of the story. Even at a young age, I was deeply impressed by the type of faithful commitment the family showed in following a call to missions in China. Reading *Where the Cotton Grows* has brought so much more richness to my understanding of who Robert and Dorothy Vick were and the influences that shaped them. We often talk about the "call of God" as an individual experience—one person being picked out by God and sent on a particular path. But the reality is that the ground is prepared by family, friends, church, and life experience to make one ready to hear the call and, even more so, to accept the call.

This story focuses on Robert and Dorothy, of course, but it raises to equal importance the stories of their parents and grandparents, their early church lives, and their school experiences that set them on this path. It then shows the legacy that path gave to their son, Paul, who continues to follow the call of God in his life today. May we all have the opportunity to be part of the foundation for others to hear how God is calling them into mission and ministry as well. I give thanks for the life of the Vicks, past, present, and future, and how they are the hands and feet of Christ in the world.

—**Rev. Dr. Sandra L. DeMott Hasenauer**
Executive Minister, American Baptist Churches
of the Rochester/Genesee Region

WHERE
THE COTTON
GROWS

WHERE THE COTTON GROWS

*A missionary calling leads a Baptist family
on a fateful journey to China leaving
a lasting legacy*

Paul Ashton Vick

The Paul A. Vick Management Trust
Rochester, NY | 2021

Where the Cotton Grows: A Missionary Calling Leads a Baptist Family
on a Fateful Journey to China Leaving a Lasting Legacy
By Paul Ashton Vick

©2021 Paul Ashton Vick

Library of Congress Control Number: 2021908077
ISBN 978-1-7370781-1-1 Hardback
ISBN 978-1-7370781-0-4 Paperback
ISBN 978-1-7370781-2-8 Ebook

Cover and book design by Susan Welt

Publisher's Cataloging-In-Publication Data
(Prepared by The Donohue Group, Inc.)

Names: Vick, Paul Ashton, author.
Title: Where the cotton grows : a missionary calling leads a Baptist family on
      a fateful journey to China leaving a lasting legacy / Paul Ashton Vick.
Description: Rochester, NY : The Paul A. Vick Management Trust, 2021.
Identifiers: ISBN 9781737078104 (paperback) | ISBN 9781737078111
      (hardcover) | ISBN 9781737078128 (ebook - ePub)
Subjects: LCSH: Vick, Paul Ashton. | Baptists--United States--Biography. |
      Clergy--United States--Biography. | Missionaries--China. |
      Airplane crash survival--China. | Aircraft accidents--China. | LCGFT:
Autobiographies.
Classification: LCC BX6495.V42 A3 2021 (print) | LCC BX6495.V42 (ebook)
      | DDC 286.1092--dc23

This book is dedicated to *Emma Ashton Vick,*
our wild and loving one, who, during her
all too short time with us, deeply touched our hearts
and is very much interwoven into the fabric of our lives.
2013–2015

Teddy Vick, age 3, in front of the For of Such is the Kingdom of Heaven *sculpture at Forest Lawn Memorial Park in Glendale, California.*

Contents

Foreword

The plane was carrying local Chinese passengers as well as American and Canadian missionaries from Shanghai to West China where they would be working. The shocking news of the airplane's tragic crash in rural China would be reported in newspapers across the United States from Maine to Florida. From Waco, Texas to Billings, Montana. From Los Angeles to Spokane. And from Vancouver and Saskatoon in Canada to Sydney, Australia and beyond.

The only passengers found alive at the crash site were 29-year-old Rev. Robert Vick and his 16-month-old son. Before breathing his last, the severely injured father was able to give instructions concerning his son. Paul Vick, the lone survivor; he was to be sent into the care of his family in Rochester, New York.

Paul's gripping narrative of that fateful flight includes recollections from pilots who had flown the same dangerous route and had known the pilot who died with his passengers. Even more intimate are the details Paul heard from Chinese farmers who witnessed the crash and rushed to the site near the remote village of Peng Bay. Equally riveting is the account of the pilot whose courage and ingenuity enabled Paul's evacuation from the town of Tianmen, which had no landing field.

Where the Cotton Grows is not simply a touching memoir for the author's children, grandchildren, and those after them. It is a fascinating read for anyone interested in the history of mission in China and in the meaning of family in one's life.

Who was Paul's family?

Paul introduces his great-grandparents, grandparents, uncles, aunts, and cousins who provided the context for his parents' faith and discernment of their call to missionary service in China. His family's interwoven lives nurtured his own. Paul later grew to know that his family was not limited to biological relatives but included people of faith in his local church, across the nation, and in far-distant lands. His parents' missionary appointment had transformed missionaries, staff, the board, and supporters of International Ministries into meaningful family members. Very movingly, Paul writes about the day he received both a Chinese name and adoption into the family of Peng Bay village.

What is family? How do those varied relationships offer opportunities to affirm one another's value? To what extent should one measure the worth of a life by its length? What are the right questions to ask concerning one's own life and the lives of others? *Where the Cotton Grows* gives readers a dramatic story that invites them to reflect on their own lives with courage and grace.

—Reid S. Trulson
Executive Director, retired
American Baptist International Ministries
March 13, 2021

PART I

THE CRASH

Chapter 1

January 28, 1947

At long last the day arrived. After two-and-a-half years of waiting and a lifetime of preparation and anticipation, Robert and Dorothy Vick stood on the tarmac at Shanghai Airport in China, their eyes fixed on the small plane that would take them to where they would start the life to which God was calling them. A China National Aviation Corporation (CNAC) C-46 sat still in the early morning hours of that cold wintry day, waiting for passengers to board and handlers to stow their baggage. Slowly my parents, carrying my brother and me, and the other passengers made their way across the tarmac and climbed the stairs of the converted cargo plane. During World War II, the C-46 had been part of a fleet of planes navigating the treacherous airpath known as "the Hump" across the Himalayas from India to provide supplies to China.

Although the war with Japan had been over for nearly two years, China was locked in an epoch civil war between the nationalist government and the communists, a war that was diverting resources from rebuilding China's infrastructure. To reach the interior of China by boat would take months. The missionaries didn't want to wait that long to begin their work.

Still, flying was extremely hazardous. During the prior six weeks, no fewer than five of the CNAC planes had crashed, three the day after

Christmas. There seemed to be no good alternative. The only other passenger service was the more costly flights run by the Lutheran Society in China. CNAC provided the only reasonably priced passenger service in China. My parents, Robert and Dorothy Vick, undoubtedly were thinking of the dangers and risks of flying as they entered the plane with their two young sons. But the weather was clear, and the prior crashes had occurred during bad weather. Capt. John Papajik was a seasoned pilot, having served as a captain in the U.S. Air Force 14th Division during World War II. He had flown many missions over the Hump between India and China, bringing goods over the Himalayas to Kunming and other cities in western China. After the Air Force discharged him on July 1, 1946, CNAC immediately hired him as one of its pilots. He was married with a young daughter, Virginia. The co-pilot, Loh Wei, and the radio operator, Y.S. Chiu, were also veterans of flying. Many other flights had successfully flown to Chungking, the destination of Flight 145, without incident. The missionaries would then secure passage by boat or plane to Chengdu where West China

CLOCKWISE FROM TOP RIGHT,
Capt. John Papajik with his wife; an example of the plane's interior after it was converted from carrying cargo during World War II to ferrying passengers; the CNAC logo used in the 1940s; a C-46 aircraft from the 1940s.

Union University was located. Established in 1905 by four Protestant mission organizations, including the American Baptist Foreign Mission Society (ABFMS), the university provided advanced education primarily in the field of medicine and dentistry but also in general liberal arts. Newly arrived missionaries would undergo intensive study in the local dialect and cultural environment in which they would live. This would be an important part of their journey, which would eventually take them to the remote city of Yipin.

My mother, 25 years old, found the seats assigned to her and my brother, Teddy, who had just turned 3. My father, age 29, settled himself and me, age 16 months, into the seats directly behind my mother and brother. As my father looked around the cabin, he observed the other passengers finding their seats. There was Beatrice Kitchen, a missionary of the United Church of Canada, who was also traveling to Chungking and then on to Chengdu to join her husband, Rev. John Kitchen. Her daughter, Muriel Tonge, had flown to Chungking the day before. Beatrice had been scheduled on the earlier flight with Muriel, who was pregnant and likely to deliver at any time. Dr. Cresswell, an American Baptist missionary serving a hospital in Yipin, had exchanged seats with Beatrice, so she could travel with Muriel in the event there was a premature delivery. Beatrice was an artist and illustrator who had created many books depicting the life of families in West China over the more than twenty years she and her family had lived in Chengdu.

Also finding their seats were Edith Meller with her three sons, 1-year-old Phillip, 5-year-old Peter, and 7-year-old Paul, who were joining her husband, Rev. Frank Meller, who was serving in Chengdu as part of the China Inland Mission. His family had been spending time back home in Canada visiting family, and he eagerly awaited their return.

As my father observed these fellow ambassadors of Christ, he thought about how close they had all become during the weeks leading to this day. During the long voyage on the *Marine Lynx*

One of the drawings from the Christmas Greetings booklet by Beatrice Kitchen.

5

from San Francisco, Beatrice and Edith shared their experience living in Chengdu, giving my parents a deeper understanding of what lay ahead for them and their children. Now that my parents actually were beginning the last leg of that journey, their excitement and anticipation grew, knowing that they would have the opportunity to strengthen these friendships, serving together in this remote area of China.

Fifteen other passengers, all Chinese, also boarded the plane. After all passengers had taken their seats, a crew member closed the heavy door to the cabin.

The first of the plane's twin propellers began to slowly turn, sputtering and coughing until it finally ignited and began to spin faster and faster, and then sprung to life with a deafening roar. Soon the second propeller also started to slowly turn, and following the same course of the first propellor, the engine roared into full action. The plane began to vibrate and shake as the power of the engines, seeking to surge the plane forward, fought against the brakes keeping the plane at a standstill. Finally, at 9:00 a.m. on January 28, 1947, my parents' commitment to God's call to be missionaries began to be realized as the plane started to taxi toward the runway.

Reaching the runway, the plane slowly turned and stopped, waiting for the tower to give final approval for takeoff. When given, the engines screamed to a higher pitch as the throttle was opened up. Both my parents instinctively hugged my brother and me as neither of us had flown before. The brake was released and the plane jolted forward, picking up speed. With engines screaming at an even higher pitch and the ground passing by faster and faster, the plane raced down the runway. Suddenly the wheels left the ground and the plane was airborne. The airport began to recede from sight. As the plane gained elevation, the plane began to buck and shake as it fought the wind and air currents it was propelling through on that cold winter day.

INSIDE THE PLANE, the air remained chilly with no perceptible heat, similar to the temporary residences the passengers had just left. They had come prepared, wearing several layers of clothing. They were especially thankful they had done so as the plane rose higher and the temperature dropped even lower. The sky was blue with few clouds, allowing the brilliance of the sun to stream through the small windows. The plane finally leveled off at a few thousand feet, giving my family a clear view of the changing landscape below. With the terror of taking off now behind us, my brother and I pressed our noses to the windows, captivated by this bird's-eye view of the world below and the cloud formations that periodically passed by. Awe and excitement replaced our initial fear. Even the plane's shaking and sudden movements as it hit air pockets and downdrafts could not dampen for long the thrill of the ride.

The adults on the plane began to relax. Quiet conversation in both English and different Chinese dialects replaced the silence of apprehension. Beatrice passed around to the other missionaries the sketches she had been working on of children and families in the Chengdu area. She was compiling a book of these illustrations that conveyed the beauty of these farming families and the simplicity of life they led. My father was particularly interested in the stories she shared, as he had been educated at Cornell University's School of Agriculture and would eventually be working with families much like those depicted in the sketches. Both Beatrice and Edith shared experiences of life in Chengdu, especially for their children, which was of great interest, particularly for my mother. Both were looking forward to their return to Chengdu and anxious to be reunited with their husbands, and in Beatrice's case, also her daughter.

Time seemed to fly by as quickly as the landscape over which they were flying. Deep in conversation, they were startled when an announcement came over the intercom that the plane was approaching the Hankow airfield for refueling. The passengers quieted down as anxiety began to well up again as the plane descended and lost air speed. Buildings became more distinguishable as the ground raced up to meet the plane. It landed with a jolt, and then lifted off the ground before once again settling onto the runway. The wing flaps came down and the passengers could almost feel the pilot apply the brakes as the plane lost speed, finally slowing to a crawl before reaching the end of the runway. There was a noticeable sigh of relief of all on board as the plane slowly turned and taxied toward the terminal.

Upon reaching the gate, the plane came to a stop, and the propellers slowed their whirring and came to a standstill. It would be a short stop, just enough time for the plane to refuel and allow one of the four crew to leave and a few new passengers to come aboard. Unable to leave the plane's tight confines, the passengers simply got out of their seats to stretch and walk up and down the aisle.

The letter A marks the site where the plane carrying the missionaries crashed in a remote area about ninety miles west of Hankow, China. Residents of the nearby village of Peng Bay rescued the only survivors, Robert Vick and son Paul, who were found lying in a cotton field near the plane's wreckage.

As the new passengers arrived, the missionaries on board were surprised and pleased to see Bishop Schuyler Garth and his wife, Lola, enter the cabin. Bishop Garth was on assignment from the Methodist Council of Bishops to gather information as to the needs of the mission sites supported by the Methodist church. In Shanghai, these missionaries from different Christian denominations had become friends in a common cause. The Garths had flown out of Shanghai bound for Chungking two weeks before. The Garths explained to the startled missionaries that Lola had become ill on the flight to Hankow, and she had to be taken off the plane for medical treatment. Now recovered, she and her husband came aboard to complete the trip to Chungking.

After everyone took their seats, and a crewman closed the heavy cabin door, once again the engines roared to life. Having made it this far without incident, the passengers felt less apprehension as the plane taxied to the runway and, after receiving clearance from the tower, sped down the runway and once again lifted off, quickly gaining altitude. The missionaries turned their attention to discuss how best to travel to Chengdu, either by boat or plane, from Chungking. About forty minutes into the flight, when the plane was around ninety miles west of Hankow, passengers on the left side of the plane began to cry out that flames were shooting out of the left engine. In a panic, my mother grabbed my

TOP *An ariel view of the crash site near Peng Bay village also shows the Piper Cub flown by Red Holmes. Once Holmes learned that Robert and Paul Vick had been taken to Tianmen, he flew the Cub there.* BOTTOM *A close-up of the wreckage of CNAC 145 shows how the plane split apart upon landing; before the crash, the plane's left wing was consumed by fire and fell into the river.*

LEFT *More wreckage of CNAC 145.* RIGHT *The remains of the plane's left engine that caught fire, causing an explosion that ripped the left wing off and caused the plane to spin and somersault out of control.*

brother, and my father grabbed me. Suddenly an explosion ripped the left wing off, and the plane began spinning and somersaulting as the pilots struggled to gain control in an effort to land on the belly of the plane.

Consumed by pure terror, passengers were at first riveted to their seats, paralyzed by the sight of the burning engine with flames quickly spreading across the wing. The explosion jolted the passengers, throwing them about the plane as it spun in circles and began plunging toward earth. Somehow, a crewmember reached the rear cargo door, and with herculean effort, pulled it open. The force of the plane's spinning began to suck objects out of the plane, including some passengers. There were no parachutes on board. My mother, arms wrapped around Teddy, and my father, grasping me, looked on in horror as other passengers began to jump or fall out of the open door. Somehow, my parents made their way to the door. Holding on to the inside of the fuselage with all their might, they looked in horror as the ground was quickly coming up to meet them. Knowing there was no alternative, they looked into each other's eyes one last time and then jumped, each tightly gripping a child, into the arms of God.

Chapter 2

Rescue

The young teenage girl walked along the road on her way home. Her parents had asked her to run some errands in a nearby village, and they expected her to return by early afternoon. She made her way toward the Peng River, watching for the ferry that would take her across to her village of Peng Bay. There was no bridge, and the only way to cross the river was by a ferry pulled across the river by a rope. In the distance, she saw the ferry leaving the other side of the river. As she quickened her pace to reach the dock before the ferry arrived, she heard in the distance the sound of an airplane.

As the plane flew closer, the sound began to change. Suddenly there was a loud explosion. Startled, she turned to see the plane on fire, spinning out of control and headed toward her village. The plane began to disintegrate, with parts being torn loose and falling into the river. She watched in horror as the burning plane continued toward her village. The plane disappeared over the trees on the other side of the river. Seconds later, she heard a thunderous crash like no sound she'd ever heard. Terrified, the girl raced to the river and pleaded with the ferryman to take her across. The moment the ferry docked, she jumped out and ran toward the village. As she drew closer, she saw complete pandemonium. People were running about shouting, trying to understand what had happened. As the girl started toward the field beyond the village, she could see flames leaping into the air. Other villagers blocked her path and told her it was too dangerous to go further.

*   *   *

Not long before the crash, several farmers had been preparing the field for planting that year's crops of rice and cotton. The sky was clear and the temperature was mild, creating ideal conditions for work. At mid-day, they left the field to eat their simple lunch. Just as they were finishing, they heard the sound of an airplane approaching. Suddenly there was an explosion. They raced out of the village in time to see a wing of the plane fall toward the river bordering their village. They watched in horror as first objects and then people were either being thrown out or jumping out of an open hatch on the side of the plane. The falling plane was headed toward the field they had been working in and were about to return to. Momentarily stunned, the farmers stood motionless as the plane crashed into their field. Suddenly it dawned on them that they might be able to rescue survivors, and they ran toward the burning fuselage. Armed only with shovels, they began to throw dirt at the plane but soon stopped as the fire raged out of control and the heat was too oppressive. They gave up hope of saving anyone who might still be inside the plane.

They turned their attention to searching the field. Bodies of men, women, and children were strewn everywhere. Body after body they came upon was lifeless, and they began to despair of finding any survivors. Suddenly one of the farmers shouted that he had found a small child next to a man, both of whom miraculously seemed to be breathing. The man was groaning and in obvious pain. The young child lay in the mud of the field with his eyes open, but he made no sound. The farmers, recognizing the urgency of getting the man and child to safety, gathered materials to make rough stretchers and carried them to the field. Very gently, the farmers, not knowing the extent of the injuries, slid the man and the child carefully onto the stretchers.

Word had spread to the village that two survivors had been found, and one of the survivors was a small child. The young girl watched as the man and the child were carried into the village. She was shocked to see that the child looked not more than a year old. As the stretcher carrying the child passed by her, she suddenly knew what needed to be done. The sister-in-law of one of the farmers carrying the stretcher had just lost a child but was still able to breast feed. She yelled out to the farmer to take the child to his sister-in-law who could provide nourishment and care. Quickly considering the options, the farmer agreed, and with the girl following, they made their way to the sister-in-law's house. Upon seeing the child, not much older than the one she had just lost, her heart melted. With tears running down her face, she carefully took the child from the stretcher and into her arms.

The man, who was in extreme pain, was taken to the home of the village healer and given medicines and herbs to lessen the pain. A search of his clothes discovered identification papers indicating he was an American. Other identification confirmed that the child was his son. The healer knew that the man was suffering from internal injuries and would die if he did not receive medical treatment beyond what he was able to provide. The closest medical facility was located in a small Catholic mission in the town of Tianmen, about fifteen miles from Peng Bay village. The fastest way to reach Tianmen was by sampan. One of the villagers volunteered to go, and he quickly left for the mission.

FATHER MICHAEL MCCARTHY WAS BORN and raised in Ireland. Ever since he could remember, his dream had been to become a priest in the Catholic Church as a way to serve God. Supported by his family, he attended seminary and took his final vows in 1931. He joined the St. Columban's Foreign Mission Society, expecting to be sent to South America as a missionary. The church, however, had other plans. His superiors were considering opening a new mission in West China, and they decided that this newly ordained priest was the perfect candidate. His

Father Michael McCarthy stands at the gate to the mission in Tianmen where Robert and Paul Vick were taken for medical care at the clinic.

assignment was to travel to a remote village known as Tianmen and establish a mission there. Arriving in 1931, he went to work. Over the years a chapel, a school, and a medical clinic were built, providing health care and education where heretofore none existed. After sixteen years of service, Father McCarthy knew that his time in China was coming to an end. His health was beginning to fail, and the war raging between the nationalist government and the communists created an uncertain future. Father McCarthy, however, was determined to stay as long as he could. He felt a deep affection and love for the people he served, and he knew how vital the medical and educational services were to this area of Hunan province.

January 28, 1947 had been a beautiful day. The sky had been clear and the weather mild. There had been no serious medical emergencies, and classroom instruction had gone well. Toward late afternoon, Father McCarthy's meditation was interrupted by a commotion outside. He went out to investigate and heard the news of the downed plane near the Peng Bay village, and that survivors who were foreigners had been found. At least one was critically wounded. Father McCarthy immediately contacted the mayor of Tianmen to inform him of the accident and the need to get to the village as quickly as possible. Soldiers near the village were summoned, and a boat large enough for an evacuation set off for Peng Bay.

*   *   *

The air tower controllers at the Chungking airport were becoming concerned. CNAC Flight 145 had taken off from the Hankow Airport on schedule around noon after refueling but radio contact had been lost soon after. Within the prior four days, another CNAC flight had been lost in the Chungking area and was still missing. There had been four other crashes of CNAC flights in previous weeks, and the controllers didn't want to believe that yet another flight might have crashed. They knew that Capt. Papajik was highly skilled, having flown over the Hump with the 14th Air Force Squadron Transport Section under the command of Gen. Claire Chennault during World War II, becoming a legend among his peers. The weather conditions had been ideal for flying, so there was hope that a disaster had been avoided. A search plane took off to try and locate the plane. The sickening sight of the crash, seen from above, dashed that hope. Parts of the plane including a wing were spread over a half-mile from the badly burned fuselage, which sat resting in a field. The search plane pilot reported back that it was extremely unlikely that any of the crew or passengers could have survived such devastation. Because of the rough terrain, it might take several days to transport a rescue crew to the crash site, but a jeep convoy was ordered to set out.

*   *   *

News of the crash began to hit the wire services around the world, and radio stations in the United States and Canada began broadcasting the unthinkable. Initial stories reported that it was extremely likely that all twenty-eight passengers and crew had died. Word began to filter into the office of the American Baptist Foreign Mission Society in Shanghai that something had gone wrong with the flight to Chungking. The plane was overdue, and all radio contact had ceased soon after takeoff from Hankow. A call placed to CNAC headquarters in Shanghai confirmed that the plane was missing, and that a search was underway. By mid-afternoon, the worst fears were realized. The plane had crashed in a remote area of China, and it was doubtful there were any survivors. The news was met with shock and disbelief. Robert and Dorothy Vick were well known within the missionary community. Their commitment and passion to the call to serve in China had touched the hearts of many during their brief stay in Shanghai. It was unthinkable that these vital young people together with their children had died before they were able to begin their service.

*   *   *

The boat carrying the soldiers arrived at Peng Bay about an hour after leaving Tianmen. Some of the soldiers hurried to the crash site where they were met with a scene of total devastation and destruction. Bodies of men, women, and children were strewn all over the field among debris from the plane. Realizing there was nothing that could be done for the victims, the soldiers began searching for identification. The bodies inside the burned-out fuselage were beyond recognition. Those lying in the field, including a young woman still clutching a child, and who were later identified as my mother and brother, were laid side by side. There were a total of twenty-six bodies including four children and the crew.

In the village, residents led soldiers to the home where my father had been taken. My father was conscious, but writhing in extreme pain. I was located in the home of the young mother. My hair was singed, and I had cuts and abrasions with partial facial paralysis. My eyes were open, although I made no sound. Not knowing the full extent of the injuries to either my Father and me, and having no ability to offer medical treatment other than for pain relief, the villagers made arrangements to transport us to the boat as quickly as possible. Stretchers were brought, and we were gently placed on them. Soldiers carrying the stretchers, accompanied by villagers, made their way to the boat. Other soldiers were left to remove the bodies from the field and guard them until a decision could be made as to their disposition.

Four hours later, the boat carrying my father and me arrived in Tianmen around 9:00 p.m. and we were immediately transported to the medical clinic where Father McCarthy was waiting for us. The medical staff quickly determined that my father was suffering from internal injuries so severe that the clinic, with its limited resources, could not adequately treat him. My father, who was in obvious agony, was told that his wife and older son had died and that he likely would not survive much longer, but his younger son's injuries did not appear to be life-threatening, and there was every reason to believe that he would survive. My father refused to take pain medication so he could remain as alert as possible to ensure that I was provided for.

DURING THE NEXT FORTY HOURS, Father McCarthy stayed by my father's side, ministering to him as best as he could. My father would slip in and out of consciousness. While conscious, although in extreme pain, he would dictate instructions to Father McCarthy asking that I be returned to my grandparents in Rochester, New York. Those times my father was conscious, I was brought to him and placed by his side. Even though I continued to make no sound, I would reach for my father and hold onto him. Father McCarthy observed that there seemed to be unspoken communication between us that brought a sense of peace to both of us. In the early morning hours of January 30th, my father slipped deeper into unconsciousness, passing away around 4:00 a.m.

Father McCarthy later sent the following account to my grandparents:

> *Please do not thank me for the very little I did or could do for your good missionary. It was a source of consolation and edification for me to assist him. He suffered much from the time of the crash until he expired, yet never once did I hear him utter a word of complaint. He knew that his wife and child were killed, but even this sad news left him calm and resigned to the will of God. He was most grateful for the least kindness shown him or the smallest service rendered to him. He thanked me again and again. For an hour or two before the end, his pain grew to an agony. The Christians recited special prayers. Towards the break of day he became unconscious and soon passed quietly away. May his soul rest in peace.*
>
> *About the circumstances of the deaths of Mrs. Vick and her older child, I have very little definite news. The crash occurred about eight miles from Tien Men City. It is certain that they were not burned. Apparently when the engine caught fire, Rev. Vick took charge of the younger child, Paul, while Mrs. Vick held the older in her arms. About three hundred yards from the crash, the left wing, left engine, and left stabilizer broke off. The plane then did several turns and somersaults and just before the crash, those who were still alive either jumped from the plane or (and more probably) were thrown through the open door.*
>
> *Rev. Vick and young child were picked up close to the plane on the left. His left arm, face, and hands were bleeding slightly. His hair was scorched. His stomach was injured. Otherwise, he seemed not in grave danger. Poor Mrs. Vick was found on the opposite side of the plane with her dead child clasped to her bosom.*
>
> *That is about all I can find out. The news is sad and tragic in the extreme, but still they were spared the worse fate of burning. May the good God grant them eternal rest. May He console their families, friends, and their brother and sister missionaries. You all have my heartfelt sympathy and prayers.*
>
> *Very sincerely yours,*
> *M. McCarthy*

Chapter 3

Evacuation

R.S. Holmes Jr., assistant chief pilot for CNAC, was in the corporation's administrative offices when word came that Flight 145 had lost radio contact and was overdue in Chungking. Red, as he was known, had flown more than 600 crossings over the Hump. Pilots would joke that the landmarks by which they flew were the crashed remains of planes that did not make it. Red knew Capt. Papajik and had full confidence in his piloting skills. The weather, for once, had been cooperative so there was no reason to be overly concerned. That soon changed when word finally came that a search plane had discovered the plane wreckage in a rural field near the village of Tianmen. After the initial reaction of shock and disbelief that yet another plane had gone down, Red began to grapple with the logistical nightmare of how to reach the crash site. It would take several days to reach the crash site by road, and CNAC's planes were too large to land and take off in soggy rice paddy fields. As Red worked on developing a plan, the urgency of reaching the plane became critical when he learned that there were survivors who urgently needed medical help. Only a small plane had any chance of landing and taking off, but in China privately owned planes were not allowed at the time, Red recounted later.

CNAC staff began a frantic search for such a plane. A distributor for Piper Cubs in Shanghai had the only Piper Cub in China, which was there for demonstration purposes and happened to be in a hangar in Shanghai. But that created a challenge. The distance from Shanghai to Hankow was about 425 miles, and the fuel capacity of the Piper Cub was too small to reach Hankow. Plus, the government would not allow the Cub to fly more than fifteen miles from the Shanghai Airport. After considering the alternatives, the CNAC staff decided to take the Cub apart and load it onto one of CNAC's transport planes and fly it to Hankow where it could be re-assembled.

*   *   *

Word of the crash of CNAC Flight 145 started hitting the airwaves in the United States by mid-day on January 29th. My father's parents, Clarence and Ethel Vick, were in their office in downtown Rochester where they ran their insurance business. It had been some time since they had received a letter from my parents, but they understood how long it took for mail to be transported across an ocean and a continent. My grandparents had sent out a lengthy letter the prior week but knew it would most likely not reach my parents for another several weeks. They had heard that my parents had secured seats on a plane that was to take them to Chungking where they would obtain passage by boat or plane to Chengdu. They were wondering how my brother and I were holding up after a rough crossing of the Pacific Ocean and the cold, damp weather in Shanghai. They were also anxious about travel in China in light of the number of plane crashes that had occurred. They knew they would continue to worry until their son, his wife, and their grandchildren were safely in Chengdu.

The call came mid-afternoon. One of the members of their church, knowing that my parents were due to fly to Chungking, asked my grandfather if he had heard news of another plane crash in China. With heart pounding, my grandfather turned on the radio to get more information. Initial reports were vague. The crashed remains of a plane had been discovered west of Hankow, and it was doubtful there were any survivors. Neither of my grandparents could believe that their family had been on that plane. They put in a call to the ABFMS offices in New York City to seek reassurance and were put through to Dr. Elmer Fridell, the executive director. Dr. Fridell confirmed that he had just received word about the crash, and that my parents, Teddy, and I had been on board but it was not yet clear if there were any survivors. My grandparents were stunned, and Dr. Friedel seemed to be just as shocked. He promised to keep them updated.

My mother's father, Lester Flanders, was working in the office of the flour mill he partially owned and operated in Baldwinsville, New York, west of Syracuse. He was preparing for a trip to take orders from bakeries and restaurants throughout central New York State. Although the radio was on, he was not paying close attention until he heard a report of a plane crash in China. He knew his daughter and her family were scheduled to fly out of Shanghai. He turned the radio up and immediately turned pale as he perhaps heard the same vague report as Clarence Vick had. Lester's fears that his daughter and her family were on the plane were confirmed when he made a call to the ABFMS headquarters in New York. As he hung up the phone in total shock, the phone rang and it was my father's dad wondering if he had heard the news. Both were barely able to keep their emotions in check. It was too unthinkable for them to grasp, just impossible for them to believe that these children and grandchildren of theirs, so full of life, passion, and zeal to serve their Lord, could perish

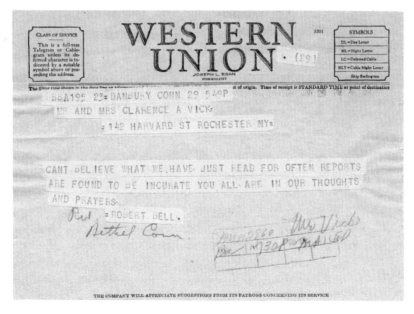

Bob Bell, a fellow seminarian of Robert Vick who had introduced him to his future wife, sent this telegram to Vick's parents expressing his disbelief and grief.

in such a manner. Both promised to keep the other informed of any new information either might receive.

As reports filtered in during the evening, the chances that there were survivors became increasingly bleak. Numb with grief, neither of my father's and mother's families were able to get much sleep. The following day, a small ray of hope materialized when they heard news that an unknown number of foreigners might have survived the crash. There was the possibility that one or more of their family might be alive.

*   *   *

The transport plane carrying the dismantled Piper Cub landed in Hankow. The question now facing Red Holmes was how to put it back together. The two mechanics at the airport had never seen a plane this small. Using their knowledge of aircraft, they reassembled the plane as best as they could. Red then took it for a test flight to see if it would fly. After Red successfully maneuvered the takeoff and landing, medical equipment was loaded onto the plane. The company doctor, Charles Hoey, boarded, and with Red in the pilot seat, the plane took off toward the crash site. Upon reaching the site, Red had difficulty finding a field large enough to set down the Cub. Once Red landed near the plane's wreckage, a note was dropped from a larger airplane accompanying the Cub. The message informed Red that the survivors had been taken to Tianmen, a walled village about fifteen miles from the crash site.

When they reached Tianmen, Red faced the same issue of where to land the plane. The fields surrounding the village appeared too small. The largest flat area was an area the size of a double basketball court inside the village wall, but it was too close to the wall to land.

As Red flew around the outskirts of the city, he spotted a field that he thought would be suitable, about a mile from the village. The plowed field was so soft that the plane stopped only ten feet after landing. Dr. Hoey took off on foot toward the village, following a foot trail and occasionally crossing a sod field, while the transport plane flying above began to drop medical supplies. Curious farmers began to materialize seemingly from everywhere. Within an hour more than 10,000 people had circled the Cub. Concerned that they might puncture the fabric covering the plane, Red kept the propeller going, blowing dust and dirt at the bystanders, and then getting out to move the tail to keep another group at bay. Shortly,

A curious crowd of thousands surrounds the Piper Cub rescue plane after Red Holmes landed it in a field near Tianmen on a mission to evacuate Paul Vick.

about 200 soldiers broke through the crowd and set up machine guns, which they fired over the heads of the crowd to keep them away.

Finally Red was able to get the first three or four rows of bystanders to sit down to keep the crowd from pushing too far forward. That solution was short-lived as the push of the throng became too great, and the human barrier had to stand to keep from getting trampled. It took more than an hour for anyone to arrive who could speak English. The crowd was becoming resentful of the soldiers. They threw clods of dirt at them and succeeded in punching several holes in the fabric of the plane. It was getting dark when a runner brought word that there was only one survivor, and that Dr. Hoey would spend the night at the mission and return with the survivor in the morning. Red moved the Cub to a safer location in the field and settled down for the night, curled up in a parachute under the plane. About 600 Chinese people also stayed throughout the night but the soldiers were able to maintain order.

Upon arrival at the mission, Dr. Hoey was met with the sad news that my father had passed away but that I appeared to be in fairly good condition. Dr. Hoey examined me and determined that my injuries most likely were not life-threatening. He had a stretcher devised that could be used to transport me to the Cub and provide a means of securing me for the plane ride to Hankow.

At sunup, Dr. Hoey arrived with two Chinese men carrying the stretcher with me strapped in. In order to lighten the plane, all supplies and equipment were removed and left in the custody of the mayor of the village. To make room for the stretcher, one set of controls also had to be removed, which of course would hamper Red's flying the Cub. Soldiers were put to work trampling down the field to create a makeshift runway. A heavy frost had fallen during the night, so ice had to be chipped away carefully from the skin fabric encompassing the Cub. Red hurried to take off, fearing the crowds again would swell in number. Red began to have doubts if the plane could generate enough speed to lift off the ground. Even though there was still too much frost on the wings and no wind to shorten the take-off, Red pulled the tail of the Cub up against a drainage ditch to create as much distance as possible before reaching the next ditch. Even though the soldiers had tried to tramp down the soil, it was still soft.

Red got back in the Cub and opened the throttle wide while standing on the brakes, and then started to take off. The Cub had just enough speed to jump the first ditch. As the Cub settled back down, the plane continued to pick up speed but unexpectedly was heading toward a four-foot-high burial mound. By that time, the Cub had just enough speed to jump the mound as it continued to pick up speed before finally lifting off.

The Cub made it safely back to Hankow. I was transferred from the makeshift stretcher to a cradle lined with blankets and then loaded onto a larger plane that Red flew back to Shanghai. Officials in CNAC's Shanghai office alerted staff in the ABFMS office confirming that my parents and Teddy had died, but I appeared to be in remarkably good condition

Dr. Charles Hoey, left, and pilot Red Holmes prepare the injured Paul Vick for his flight. Holmes flew Hoey and Vick in the tiny Piper Cub to Hankow, and then in a larger plane to Shanghai for delivery to Country Hospital.

and had safely been evacuated from Tianmen and was en route to Shanghai. Dr. Hoey learned that I should be taken to Country Hospital upon arrival, where he and I would be met by medical staff retained by ABFMS.

This update was quickly forwarded to the New York office of ABFMS, which in turn immediately called both sets of grandparents with news of my survival and evacuation to Country Hospital. From all reports, I appeared to have suffered no serious injury.

By all accounts, Paul Vick received excellent medical care for his two broken legs and slight paralysis at Country Hospital in Shanghai.

My grandparents also learned that a letter from Father McCarthy had been given to Dr. Hoey and would be forwarded as soon as possible. It provided details of the crash and my father's last hours and contained instruction as to my care.

The bodies of my parents and brother, as well as the remains of the other missionaries and children who had died in the crash, were taken to Hankow. All their families decided that the missionaries' remains should be buried in China, the place to which God had called them. They were eventually interred in the International Cemetery, forever becoming a part of a land they loved.

*　　　*　　　*

The crash of Flight 145 made international news undoubtedly because of the American and Canadian missionaries on board. A headline blared from the *China Daily Tribune* on January 29, 1947: "**Second CNAC Missing Plane Found Near Hankow; Fate of 12 Missionaries Unknown.**" The story went on to state:

> "CNAC airline No. 145, with 26 passengers and crew aboard, which disappeared on a Shanghai-Chungking flight shortly after noon yesterday, has been found about 100 miles from Hankow, officials of the airline revealed at noon today.

"Initial information received by the CNAC head office gives no details concerning the fate of passengers, among whom are 12 foreigners, all members of various missionary organizations. … Plane No. 145 took off from Lunghwa Airfield at 7 a.m. yesterday and made Hankow safely at 11:15 a.m. where it took on another four passengers, two of them Bishop and Mrs. Garth.

"The plane was 30 minutes' flight out of Hankow when it lost radio contact with the Wuhan airfield…The airline, according to company officials, was expected in Chungking at 2:15 p.m. yesterday. A crash was feared when no news of the plane was heard at a late hour last night."

The story goes on to detail that the managing director of CNAC and its chief pilot were on their way to Hankow, and that the other CNAC plane that had gone missing a week ago still had not been found. The article also included names of the missionaries on board, including "Mr. and Mrs. Robert A. Vick, Rochester, New York, and their two children, Paul, 10 months, and Theodore, three years. The Vicks are from the China Inland Mission and were reported on their way to open a mission in Chengdu."

An article written by Walter G. Rundle, a United Press Correspondent, appeared the next day in the *China Daily Tribune* with the all-capitalized headline: "PASSENGERS OF CNAC PLANE NO. 145 BELIEVED DEAD; WRECK SEEN NEAR HANKOW."

The story led with:

"Officials of the China National Aviation Corporation yesterday afternoon expressed the fear that the 27 persons aboard its airline No. 145, including 12 American and Canadian missionaries, have perished…Definite information concerning the fate of the passengers, however, waits reports from a jeep convoy which has been rushed to the scene of the crash."

A later report states that the plane lost radio contact with Hankow seventeen minutes after taking off at 11:15 a.m., and the wreckage was discovered at Chaoshih, sixty miles west of Hankow. "Central News reported form Hankow that all occupants—26 altogether, including the pilot, co-pilot, and radio operator—except one foreigner—were killed. The foreigner was severely wounded."

AT TOP *Chapel at the International Cemetery in Hankow where the missionaries and their children killed in the plane crash were buried at the request of all the families.* ABOVE LEFT *Dorothy and Teddy Vick were buried together on the left, with Robert Vick on the right.* ABOVE RIGHT *This headstone marks the graves of the Vick family.*

Back in New York State, newspapers from Rochester to New York City began reporting that my family was missing, and later that I was the only survivor. Many articles featured a photo of my family that had been taken shortly before the trip. My parents sit smiling, with a grinning Teddy on my father's lap, and me with a more pensive look on my mother's lap. My grandparents saved clippings that included not just the

Rochester newspapers, but places where my father had preached, such as Albion and Binghamton, and in Baldwinsville, the hometown of my mother. Headlines included **"The Rev. R.A. Vick and family missing on Chinese plane"** and **"Rochester family lost in disaster"** and then when my survival was known: **"Infant survives leap in dad's arms from fiery plane"** and **"Miracle baby only survivor of plane crash."**

A United Press story printed in the *Times-Herald* in Washington, D.C., on February 1, 1947 was headlined: **"Tale of heroism bared in fatal airplane crash."** It read:

> "An American couple made a heroic effort to save the lives of their two small children by leaping from a flaming airliner seconds before it crashed Tuesday, 90 miles west of Hankow, the United Press learned today. In a final statement before he died, Robert A. Vick of Rochester, N.Y., told how he and Mrs. Vick picked up their two small sons and jumped from the burning airliner.

> "Vick saved the life of his 10-month-old son, Paul, the only survivor among the 27 passengers and crew members aboard the plane. Mrs. Vick and 3-year-old Theodore Vick were killed. The heroic father died at 4 a.m. yesterday in a small hospital near the village of Tiernmun (sic), where the plane crashed, after dictating his statement and asking that the baby be sent to his grandparents in the United States."

The story went on to state that Dr. Hoey had returned to Shanghai with me and that I had suffered two broken legs and other injuries but was expected to recover with no permanent injury.

*   *   *

Whether the plane crash was the result of carelessness or deliberate sabotage is a mystery that may never be solved. Authorities who investigated the crash determined that after the plane was refueled in Hankow, the gas cap was either intentionally or accidentally left off. The absence of the cap allowed fuel to flow into the engine and cause the explosion.

Chapter 4

Convalescence and Return Home

My journey begins in a real sense when I was taken from the Mission at Tianmen and flown back to Shanghai. My father, mother, and brother, the only family I had known, were gone. Although I was alone in a strange land and surrounded by strangers, from accounts recorded at the time, there seemed to be a peace that had descended over me. Country Hospital became my home for the next two months. Both of my legs were broken. A photo on the front page of *The North-China Daily News* in Shanghai shows my tiny body with both legs elevated in traction. The photo caption from the English-language newspaper of Monday, February 3, 1947 stated:

> *"Sandy-haired, blue-eyed, 17-month-old Paul Vick, sole survivor of the CNAC plane crash beyond Hankow on January 28, which caused the death of 25 persons aboard, is shown here in his room at Country Hospital in Shanghai, his broken legs suspended by pulleys. Paul's parents, Baptist missionaries from Cheshire, Conn., and Rochester, N.Y., and his one-year-old brother, Theodore, were among those who lost their lives." (Note that Teddy's age is incorrect.)*

By this time, the paralysis had disappeared, and my other injuries, primarily contusions and abrasions, healed quickly.

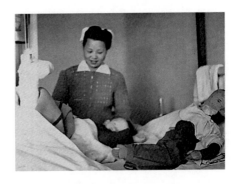

Nurse Liu (pictured), along with Nurse Sun, was charged with taking care of Paul Vick in Country Hospital.

Two Chinese nurses were assigned to care for me. An Acme Telephoto appeared in the Rochester *Democrat and Chronicle* showing a nurse by my side, my legs elevated in traction. The caption headline was "CITY YOUNGSTER... LONE SURVIVOR OF AIR CRASH." Underneath: "Here, comforted by a Chinese nurse in Country Hospital, Shanghai, is 14-month-old Paul Vick, lone survivor of an air crash near Hankow, China, in which his parents, Mr. and Mrs. Robert A. Vick of 142 Harvard St., and his brother, Theodore, 3, died with 24 other passengers and crew members. The Rochester missionaries leaped from the flaming airliner with the children in their arms, but only Paul survived. He suffered two broken legs but physicians say he will recover."

Missionaries and staff from ABFMS regularly looked in on me and reported what good spirits I seemed to exhibit in my interactions, particularly with my nurses. One of those visitors was Rev. Frank Meller, whose wife and three sons died in the crash. In a letter to the China Inland Mission, he wrote:

> *"I went to see Paul Vick...at the Country Hospital in Shanghai. He was so sweet and happy, with his two broken legs still suspended by pulleys...He looked at me with eyes of curiosity. The Chinese nurses were wonderful with him and told me that many people wanted to adopt him...Paul called his nurse Liu "umM" as she looked after him from the time he came to the Hospital. Whenever nurse Sun came around, Paul would grab her sweater and feel in her pockets. She would usually bring him candy. I don't think he remembers anything about the accident but when he hears a plane, he points at the window and says, 'see!' "*

Gordon Gilbert, another missionary and former seminary classmate of my father's, also arranged to see me. My family had visited Gordon and his wife, Jean, in Hangchow after arriving in China. In a letter dated Feb. 22, 1947, Jean, wrote to my Vick grandparents:

"Gordon went to Shanghai and saw Paul and came home feeling very good about him. Gordon says he really looks wonderful. He said his cheeks have filled out and he is cheerful and contented looking and laughs and plays quite a lot. Gordon says the hospital staff is giving him the best of care, and that they have been just stuffing food down him, and he is picking up weight. Of course, when he was here, he had had that difficult trip on the boat, and he had a little of his cold left. Gordon says Paul looks a lot better now than he did when he was here. He also said that the very slight paralysis which the specialist says is almost gone now from his face is not visible at all. At the time he said he expected it to completely disappear in another week. Gordon was so happy to see Paul looking so good."

By THE FIRST OF APRIL, the medical staff determined I was recovered sufficiently to travel back to the United States. At that time, an air route had not been established for commercial flights from Shanghai to the states, but CNAC was working on it. A test flight was being scheduled, and arrangements were made to fly me to San Francisco, a three-day trip. CNAC assigned a stewardess to travel with me. Upon landing in San Francisco, Dr. Ralph Knudsen, dean of Berkeley Baptist Divinity School, met me with his wife as well as Daisy Skoglund, wife of Dr. John Skoglund who was on the faculty of the Divinity School. Mrs. Skoglund wrote: "Today the baby came! What a darling he is. He went right to us with a big smile. He seems to feel that the whole world loves him."

Newspapers touted my arrival to the United States. One photo shows me sitting on the San Francisco Airport floor with my left hand on a suitcase, presumably mine. In another photo, I sit on a counter with a big smile on my face, looking at Daisy Skoglund and Ralph Knudsen while Mrs. Knudsen and son Mark Knudsen look on. Still another photo shows me sitting on a small chair in the Knudsen living room, clutching a Chinese doll. My eyes and mouth are wide open, seemingly happy.

I stayed with the Knudsens in Berkeley as it took about a week to arrange a flight to LaGuardia Airport in New York City. En route, the plane stopped for refueling in St. Louis. During the stop, a passenger on our flight got off the plane and shortly returned with a stuffed elephant toy and gave it to me. That passenger was Frank Sinatra. According to news reports, I had struck up quite a relationship with him on the plane, and after hearing of my story, he was inspired to do this act of kindness.

TWA stewardesses took good care of me on the flights to New York City. The *Kansas City Star* featured a photo of me sitting on the lap of stewardess Margaret Harris when the plane made a stop there. The headline read: "**HIS WINGS WON EARLY; INFANT TAKES AIR TRIP TO NEW HOME IN STRIDE; Paul Vick, 18 months old, whose parents died in China Crash is brief visitor here.**" The story reported that I had boarded the plane the night before in San Francisco, and Harris stated: "He hasn't uttered a whimper. Last night, I undressed him and put on his sleepers. He crawled up on our makeshift bed on the seat and scarcely blinked his eyes all night long."

The story went on to say I was eagerly eating animal crackers and playing with a toy dog. "The hostess this morning dressed the boy in green jumper trousers with a light green shirt, which made a colorful contrast with Paul's orange-red hair."

My father's parents, Clarence and Ethel Vick, and his sisters, Carol Henry and Ruth Happ, met the plane at LaGuardia Airport. Newspaper photographers were there to capture the moment when stewardess Isabel Ghab carried me down

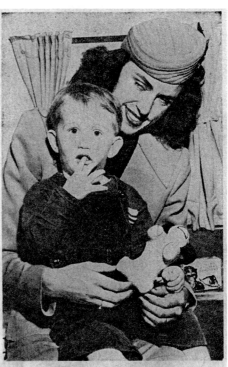

STRANGERS STILL ARE PUZZLING to red-haired Paul Vick, 18 months old, the only survivor of a plane crash January 28 in Hankow, China, who is shown here with Miss Margaret Harris, T. W. A. hostess. Paul's parents, Mr. and Mrs. Robert A. Vick, Baptist missionaries, and his 3-year-old brother, Theodore Vick, were among the twenty-five persons killed in the crash. Today the baby came through Kansas City on the last phase of a journey to New York, where he will be cared for by his grandparents, Mr. and Mrs. Clarence Vick. On the trip from Shanghai, he has been the charge of air line hostesses and the Travelers Aid society—(Kansas City Star photograph).

Airline hostesses, including Margaret Harris from Trans World Airlines (TWA), took good care of Paul Vick on the many legs of his trip from Shanghai to New York City.

31

the steps from the plane and into the arms of my grandparents. I look a little pensive in my grandfather's arms, compared to the smiles on the adults, no doubt needing a bit of time to adjust to being around more strange yet loving faces.

From New York City, we traveled by car back to Rochester, stopping in Baldwinsville to see my mother's parents. At 10:30 p.m. on April 11, 1947, I arrived at the place I would call home, 142 Harvard St. in Rochester, five long months after leaving.

LEFT *Returning to San Francisco, Paul was greeted by, from left, Daisy Skoglund; Rev. Ralph Knudson, dean of Berkeley Baptist Divinity School; Mrs. Knudson; and son Mark Knudson. Daisy Skoglund's husband, Rev. Dr. John Skoglund, later joined the faculty at Colgate Rochester Divinity School and his children were classmates of Paul at Monroe High School.* RIGHT *Paul's grandparents, Ethel and Clarence Vick, welcomed him at LaGuardia Airport in New York City. At left is Dr. Elmer Fridell, executive secretary of the American Baptist Foreign Mission Society.*

On the drive from New York City to Rochester, the Vicks stopped at the Baldwinsville home of Paul's maternal grandfather, Lester Flanders. His wife, Ester, holds a toy elephant that fellow passenger Frank Sinatra had given to Paul after meeting the toddler on the flight from San Francisco to LaGuardia Airport.

Chronicle

N. Y., SATURDAY, APRIL 12, 1947

...arence Vick is ther...
...n Paul, only surviv...
...cident in China whic...
...ssionary parents ar...

KODAKERY

NEWSPAPER FOR THE MEN AND WOMEN OF EASTMAN KODAK COMPA...

Copyright by Eastman Kodak Company, Rochester, N. Y.

Survivor of Air Tragedy in China

...perates at Home of Uncle from...

...escaping death in an
...that took the lives of
...mother and brother,
...ick is fast recuperat-
...Happ, Kodak Park

...months old, arrived
...China only recently
...the long journey by
...re of airline steward-
...ve after his father and
...eaped from the burn-
...with the children in

...ed in December

...her with his parents,
...A. Vick and his wife,
...a brother, Theodore
...here the Rev. Mr. Vick
...up duties as a Baptist
...After leaving Shang-
...ngking, their plane
...ly at Hangkow.
...miles out of Hangkow,
...the plane caught fire

Earl Happ and Paul Vick

...spin. As it neared the ground, Mrs.
Vick jumped out with Theodore

...followed with Pau...
...almost instantly exce...
...suffered two broken le...
...contusions. He wa...
Baptist Hospital a...
...light plane which wa...
the scene of the cras...
legs in traction of th...
...several weeks in bed...
...favorably to the car...
doctors and nurses...

Fun with chil...

Today he toodle
...other youngster h...
...learning to walk a...
...playtime companion of...
...children, Bobby, 3, an...
...supplemented by...
...with members of t...
Paul, too, will be ro...
...wooded grove adjoin...
...home and cutting "cu...
...dian" capers with t...

When not with his...
...and Aunt Dorothy,
Rochester with his...
Mr. and Mrs. Clar...

'HOME' AT LONG LAST

Little Paul Vick, survivor of the China plane crash t...
took the lives of his parents and brother, is shown as...
arrived here last night with his grandparents, Mr. and M...
Clarence A. Vick, with whom he will live. He clutches...
elephant Frank Sinatra gave him on one leg of long jour...

Vick Baby, Air Crash Survivor

Brought Home by Grandpare...

Little 18-month-old Paul Vick, survivor of the China...
crash which killed his missionary parents and a 3-ye...
brother, came back to Rochester last night.

Accompanied by a toy elephant presented to him by...
Frank Sinatra while en route by
air from San Francisco to LaGuardia Field, New York City, Paul arrived at 10:30 p. m. at the residence
of his grandparents, Mr. and Mrs.
Clarence A. Vick, with whom he
will henceforth live, at 142 Harvard

...a brief visit yesterday with
...maternal grandparents, M
Mrs. Lester Flanders.

Mr. and Mrs. Vick wer...
New York that little Paul...
made friends with Sinatr...
transcontinental plane. Th...
...Paul...

Chapter 5

Clarence Ashton Vick and Ethel Thompson Vick

My father, in his application to become an American Baptist Missionary, wrote: "I was born into a home where Christ was the Master. My father had always hoped to be a minister. Because of economic factors, this was not possible. Ever since I was very young, both of my parents have cherished in their hearts the hope that someday I would become a minister of Jesus Christ. They have opened every possible avenue which would lead me to this ultimate decision..."

My grandfather, Clarence Ashton Vick, was a second-generation immigrant from England. His father, Charles Vick, the youngest of eight children. was born on the ship *Ontario* in the New York harbor on October 17, 1833 while his family awaited admission to the United States. Four years later, when his father could not find suitable employment as a shoe maker, the family moved to Rochester, New York, only three years after its incorporation.

Charles' older brother James Vick had learned the printing trade and at the same time had developed a passion around horticulture. He became a printer for Frederick Douglas' *North Star* newspaper as well as horticultural magazines. His interest in horticulture initially led to experimenting with seeds, and eventually he established a seed distribution business. By the late nineteenth century, he had purportedly become the largest seed distributor in the world.

The seed business provided Charles with a job, and thus a livelihood upon which to start a family. On August 3, 1871, he married Mary Ashton, who was nineteen years younger than he. Mary's mother died when she was five years old, followed by her father thirteen years later. Charles and Mary had five children; one died in childbirth. My grandfather, Clarence, was the youngest, born on June 12, 1886. Nine years later, Charles died. Grandpa Vick was forced to leave school after eighth grade to help support his mother and sisters. He took on hard-labor jobs, including lugging a heavy bag of newspapers and delivering them, which left him permanently with stooped shoulders. The cause of his father's death, alcoholism, left Grandpa Vick a passionate proponent of prohibition.

Even though he was unable to complete his formal education, Grandpa Vick was determined to learn a trade that would provide economic opportunity, so he took classes at the Mechanic's Institute (now

Paul grew up in the family home at 142 Harvard St., Rochester, which was first purchased by the parents of his grandmother, Ethel Thompson Vick. Pictured standing at the turn of the twentieth century from left are Arabelle Ada Aides Thompson and her children Ethel, George, and Bert.

35

Members of the Thompson family at their Harvard Street home. STANDING FROM LEFT *George, Ethel, and Bert with their parents,* SEATED, *Arabelle and Frank. George lived in the home until his death.*

Rochester Institute of Technology) to learn drafting. This opened the door for him to work for the telephone company in Buffalo as well as becoming an instructor of drafting at the Mechanic's Institute on the side.

Grandma Vick's parents, Frank Thompson and Arabella Ades, married on July 27, 1871 and settled in Rochester, where Frank started a house painting and wall papering business. They had four children who survived; my grandmother was the youngest, born on January 4, 1881. The oldest child, George, joined his father in the business when he was mature enough. Frank and Arabelle Thompson eventually acquired a home on the corner of Goodman and Brighton streets in Rochester, which they eventually moved to 142 Harvard St., the location where it still stands as of this writing. George, who never married, lived there until his death.

Grandpa and Grandma Vick married in 1912. Grandpa Vick continued working at the telephone company and teaching drafting. For the first few years, they lived in a house on Mulberry Street about a mile from the Thompson home on Harvard. When Grandma Vick's parents became ill, they moved to 142 Harvard St. to care for them. Frank Thompson died in 1915, followed by Arabella in 1916.

For a period of time, Grandpa Vick continued to work in Buffalo, requiring him to take the train and stay in Buffalo during the week, then return to Rochester for the weekend. With the responsibility of caring for Grandma Vick's parents and the arrival of their first child, Ruth Arabelle, on November 1, 1915, Grandpa Vick decided he needed to work in Rochester. He went into partnership with an acquaintance to start an insurance business. Unfortunately, the partnership did not work out and the acquaintance left Grandpa Vick holding considerable debt. He worked long hours to pay off the debt, and he vowed never again to enter into a partnership.

My father, Robert, arrived on the scene on December 24, 1917. Grandma Vick hoped he would arrive on Christmas Day, but I guess he couldn't wait. Exactly five years to the day after the birth of Ruth Arabelle, Ethel Carol, the third and last child, was born.

Times were difficult financially for the Vicks. Along with paying off his business debt, Grandpa Vick had a wife and three small children to support while he worked hard to grow his business. Grandma Vick made many of their clothes, often giving them as gifts at Christmas and for birthdays. My grandparents would not have dreamed of taking a handout. In spite of the hard times, the family's needs were met. The church was central in their lives. They were steadfast members of the Park Avenue Baptist Church. In spite of meager financial resources, Grandpa and Grandma Vick were committed tithers. Even in later years, Grandpa Vick set aside ten percent of whatever he took out of the business for personal expenses and placed it in the weekly church envelope. The family lived off the rest.

The entire life of the family revolved around the church. Grandma Vick, having been a teacher, was involved with younger

Clarence and Ethel Vick raised their grandson Paul at the request made by their son, Robert, when he was critically injured in the plane crash.

children's programs and was a regular participant in quilting and sewing groups, making blankets and clothes for distribution to missions. She also served on the board of managers of the Fairport Baptist Homes, initially a residential home for aging women; her tenure lasted into the 1960s. Grandpa Vick was active in men's groups at the church and regularly volunteered in outreach programs.

IN 1917, THE PARK AVENUE BAPTIST CHURCH BUILDING was sold to a Jewish congregation, Temple Beth El, and a merger with Second Baptist Church took place, forming the East Avenue Baptist Church. My father's older sister was the last to be dedicated in the Park Avenue church before it was sold. When a majority of the East Avenue Baptist Church congregation elected to build downtown (in what became known as the Temple Building), my grandparents, with other members who were committed to establishing a church in the Park Avenue area, left to form Immanuel Baptist Church. For the first several years the church held its services at the Rochester Theological Seminary on the corner of Alexander Street and East Avenue. Several of the church's founding members were on the faculty of the seminary. Land was soon purchased on the corner of Brunswick and Park Avenue. Construction began in 1926 and was completed within the next two years. The first person to be baptized in the new church was Ruth Arabelle Vick.

At the first meeting of the newly formed church in March 1923, Grandpa Vick was elected church clerk. Establishing a new church and building a new church home took up nearly all of his time not spent on his business or family. Grandpa Vick also took on the responsibility of Sunday School superintendent. As stated by my father in his seminary application, his father had always wanted to go into the ministry but had been unable to realize that dream because he left school to support his mother and sisters. Instead, he began taking courses (such as "The Apostolic Age" and "Child Study: Pilgrim Training Course for Teachers") at the Rochester School of Religious Education. He studied scripture, ethics, and theology throughout his life.

At the beginning of one church school year, Grandpa Vick addressed those who would be leading educational instruction with the following words: "Tomorrow Sunday, September 16, has been designated among our Protestant churches as Religious Education Sunday. It is therefore

The laying of the cornerstone of the
new Immanuel Baptist Church in
1925 involved a number of dignitaries.
STANDING IN THE FOREGROUND AT LEFT
*Dr. George Cross, professor of theology
at Colgate Rochester Divinity School
and chairman of the church's board
of deacons, and Dr. John R. Slater,
chairman of the building committee.* STANDING IN THE BACKGROUND
FROM LEFT *Dr. John L. Vichert, CRDS
professor; Dr. J.W.A. Stewart, CRDS
dean; Fred Reynolds, former pastor
of Parsells Baptist Church; Dr. Alfred
Isaacs, ex-secretary, Monroe Associates;
Dr. Alfred T. Mercer, Immanuel Baptist
pastor.* AT RIGHT *Program commemorating the 20th anniversary of the
founding of Immanuel Baptist Church
at 815 Park Ave., Rochester.*

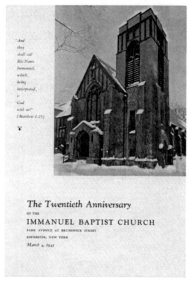

The Twentieth Anniversary
OF THE
IMMANUEL BAPTIST CHURCH
PARK AVENUE AT BRUNSWICK STREET
ROCHESTER, NEW YORK
March 4, 1941

fitting that we should consider together some goals to be strived for in
our Church School this year.

"On behalf of a most loyal and consecrated group of fellow offi-
cers, department superintendents and teachers, I wish to state that we
approach our task this year seriously, joyously, and expectantly. Seriously,

because we appreciate the responsibility that is ours as week by week we try to hold up before our pupils the Christian life as the most appropriate and satisfactory way of living and realize that these same pupils are evaluating our teaching by the simplicity of lives we lead.

"Joyously because we are working for our Master, for His church, and for those of whom he said, 'of such is the Kingdom of Heaven'.

"Expectantly because we know that He goes before us and that if we do not fail him success must crown our efforts."

As a congregational-based church, Immanuel Baptist Church depended on the financial giving of its members. During the church's earliest years, the cost to construct the new building required the raising of substantial financial resources. Immanuel Baptist Church held a number of fundraisers including the "$1 Fund." In support of this initiative, Grandpa Vick wrote the following poem:

In looking back I well can see
How oft I scarce can tell?
That by the kitchen range did stand
My mother making jell.

We children though we always played
Outdoors when we were well
Were satisfied inside to stay
If mother was making jell.

Candy and cake we dearly loved
But our spirits never fell
When homemade bread became our lot
Spread thick with mother's jell.

She sent a dollar here tonight
That much our fund to swell
And wanted me to say 'twas earned
By mother making jell.

Grandpa Vick not only was active in the church but also in the affairs of the American Baptist Union, an association of Baptist churches in the Rochester area. For nearly thirty-five years, he served as the clerk of the Permanent Council of Ordination. Generations of students seeking ordination after graduating from Colgate Rochester Divinity School received their Certificate of Ordination containing his signature. There was rarely an association event or a program at the Divinity School he did not attend.

Around 1927, Grandma Vick came down with tuberculosis. She was advised to go to a sanatorium in the Adirondack mountains. Grandma Vick was certain that the illness was fatal. After several months at the sanatorium, she refused to stay away any longer and insisted on returning home to die. Grandpa Vick told her he would remind her of what she said when she turned 80, and he did.

Integrity of behavior and respect for others, to see the good in others, were cardinal principles by which my father's parents lived their lives. Grandpa Vick often did business with a handshake. When clients were unable to pay their insurance premiums, he would often advance the money to them, having faith that it would be repaid. If someone reached out to my grandparents for help, they would immediately respond. They expressed their faith more often by what they did than what they said. Their concern was for the well-being of others, addressing need not so much by words but by actions. Grandpa Vick's admonishment to the Sunday School teachers was lived out in the living of his life. Underlying everything he did was a certain knowledge of God's unconditional love for his creation, and that there was nothing that could separate men and women from that love. This was the environment in which my father was raised; he was always encouraged to seek out God's will for his life.

Three weeks after news of the plane crash was received, Grandpa Vick wrote a letter that was sent out to the American Baptist family. In that letter he wrote: "We do not believe that God caused or directed the tragedy. This is unthinkable and inconsistent with our conception of a God of love…We cannot express our joy that Paul has been spared, that he will carry no permanent injuries, and that in due time he will be sent back to us. Having entered our sixties, Mrs. Vick and I have thus suddenly had placed in our hands the huge responsibility of bringing him up so that he will reach manhood with the same vision his father possessed. Should he, when he reaches the age of decision, show any disposition to follow his father's calling, we shall be very grateful."

Grandma Vick wrote: "We have received many beautiful letters from young people whose lives Bob has touched, as he moved among them during his camp experiences and deputation work. He thought he was marking time, waiting to go to China where he had burning zeal to serve. We know now he was accomplishing his life's work then. The work in China cannot die, it will not die. Their spirit will work through others to take up the torch where they laid it down."

Chapter 6

Lester Ellsworth Flanders and Frances Smith Flanders

My mother's father, Lester Flanders, was born on a farm about twenty miles north of Centerville, Michigan. He was the seventh of eight children, all of whom lived to adulthood except Fred, who died of illness at age 12. Grandpa Flanders told me he never saw his mother cry, but he did see tears in her eyes years later at the mention of Fred's name. His father, Calvin, was raised by a family named Case because his mother had died when he was three years old, and his father, Zoroaster Semirarius Flanders, was unable to care for him. Calvin told of "how frightened he was when a big man (Porter Case) came to the home, picked him up, and carried him off." When Calvin was 21, he married 16-year-old Ida Isabelle Lee, the daughter of Horace Otis Lee and Sarah Gilbert Lee. As a wedding present, Porter Case gave Calvin a team of horses. In a written account, Grandpa Flanders recalled about his father that "It was reported that the neighbors thought Calvin would be very successful as he was up before daylight and worked like a beaver until dark." He further commented that "From my own knowledge, as long as he was a farmer, the beavers had nothing on him. On his way to town on a lumber wagon he would sit on the edge of the seat and push on the lines…Yet he was too polite to pass another rig going in the same direction. The country roads were dusty, and one just didn't kick

Calvin and Ida Lee Flanders, the maternal great-grandparents of Paul, in the yard of their home in Sherwood, Michigan, in the 1920s

dust in another's face. (One lesson I learned from my father)."

The Case home where Calvin was raised centered its life around the Bible. Bible reading and prayer were daily experiences. When Lester and his younger sister, Letha, were about 12 and 10 years old, they spent a night in the home of Grandma Case in Colon. After breakfast, Grandma Case read the Bible and then knelt by her chair and prayed. Letha and Lester continued to sit in their chairs, not knowing how to react to the situation. After Grandma Case got up off her knees, she suggested in her very kindly way that when they were where "morning devotions" were practiced, it would be nice if they, too, knelt. Morning devotions had a strong influence on Grandpa Flanders throughout his life.

Grandpa Flanders' mother, Ida Lee Flanders, also was brought up in a Christian home. "Family devotions" were the rule and religiously maintained by her father, Horace Lee. Horace Lee believed in following the rules of the Bible, and as a result was known throughout the area as a "Good Man." Some twenty years after his father's death, Grandpa Flanders was walking along a country road near Sherwood. A man gave him a lift, and when he found out he was a descendent of Horace Lee, he told him that people of the area still spoke highly of the Good Man Horace Lee. That man who gave him a lift was the Free Methodist preacher.

There was a difference in depth of faith between Grandpa Flanders' mother and his father. His father did not accept blindly every word in the Bible as it sounded. Grandpa Flanders recounted that "he once heard his father scoff at the Bible account of Jonah and the whale. He said he didn't believe it ever happened that way. Apparently, he had not decided in his own mind a satisfactory explanation. His mother, on the other hand, accepted the Bible as the inspired word of God and never questioned any part she did not readily understand. If the Bible said it, it was good enough for her. She was happy to sing old hymns such as "There is Not a Friend Like the Lowly Jesus," "Jesus, Savior Pilot Me," and "Rock of Ages, Cleft for Me" as she worked around the house.

When she was dying, she was heard to quote from a hymn, "I would not live always, I welcome the tomb; since Jesus has lain there, I dread not its gloom." She went to sleep quietly without pain or discomfort—sustained by faith in the end.

Reflecting on his father, Grandpa Flanders wrote: "On looking back, I felt my father's first thought was for the welfare of his children. He kept them in good clothes and well fed. He wanted them to have a good education. With all the hard work on the farm, he would never have his boys stay out of school to help. He did see to it they were busy on Saturdays. Zoe (Lester's brother) and I played ball with the high school team. One Saturday, at corn planting time, the school Prof., Mr. Nevereth, came out and helped plant corn forenoon so we could play ball in the afternoon. I've known my father to wash the best buggy and polish the light harness so Zoe and I could drive out in style."

Grandpa Flanders was born at home. He wrote that "it was not the custom in those days to go to the hospital for such events. There were no telephones; the family doctor arrived (sometimes on time) and did what was necessary for five dollars. He then jotted down the name of newly arrived infant (or remembered it as best as he could) and later it was recorded in the county seat—if he didn't forget it. In my case, it was discovered after about sixty years that the record showed me to have the name Leslie Ellsworth Flanders. (Therein lies a tale.) My older sister, Lillie, was 19 years old the year I was born and given the privilege of naming me. She had married Elmer Ellsworth Overholt, who had a brother whose first name was Lester. Lillie had named me Lester

Lester Flanders, Paul's maternal grandfather, was born at home in Sherwood, Michigan. His sister chose his first name.

45

FROM LEFT *The Smith family: Lottie McHuron, Frances, Margery (seated on lap) Newton, Winifred, photographed in the early 20th century.*

Ellsworth Flanders. When I was 60 years old, I went (with my brother Zoe) to the county seat in Centerville, Michigan, to get my birth certificate. That was when we discovered the error. Zoe signed a paper which corrected the error. Strange enough, when I was a young boy, I had wished they had named me Leslie as I thought Leslie sounded better than Lester. My father was 43 when I was born and my mother 38. Since they were married in 1872, they did not need me much. Neither did they need Letha Irene who came two years later—last of the flock. However, we were welcomed and never felt neglected. In fact, I think they were glad to see us."

Grandpa Flanders attended a one-room school house in Mudsock. My grandfather wrote: "It was one and a quarter mile westward toward the village of Sherwood from the farm. The dirt roads were very muddy in the spring and dusty in the dry summer time…The girls sat on one side—the boys on the other. Way out back on the girl's side was an 'out-house' for the girls and another on the far back corner for the boys. The water pail stood on a bench inside the front door on the boy's side. In those days (before germs) a dipper was used by all. It was considered a privilege to be allowed to walk down to the nearest house to get a pail of water. Of course it took two boys (one on each side) to lug the pail of water without slopping. In the center of the room was a large heating stove, and a woodshed outside kept it supplied with fuel. It got pretty hot near the stove but not always so hot in the corners. It made a good place to dry out a boy's felt socks after breaking through the ice on a pond in a field nearby. I couldn't very well walk a mile or more in wet socks in the winter…After three or four years in Mudsock, we began driving four miles to Sherwood where my father thought the educational opportunities would be better...One large room held all four years of high school. The school principal taught all subjects in the high school...No wonder I was admitted into Michigan Agricultural College on condition I make up a few credits before I could graduate...However, before entering MAC, I went back to Mudsock after high school and taught for a year at forty dollars a month with two dollars thrown in for doing my own janitorial work. I didn't particularly like sweeping the dusty school room as there was no such thing as a sweeping compound in those days. I hired one of the big girls to sweep for me. For pay, she got a five-cent bag of peanuts. No sweeping compound—no minimum wage law."

Grandpa Flanders commented that it was the busiest year he ever put in; he taught twenty-five to thirty youngsters and seven grades. By the following year he had saved $300 that saw him through the first year of MAC (now known as Michigan State University) in East Lansing. By working summers and borrowing money from his brother, he declared that he had struggled through four years at MAC and had come out with a diploma and a firm conviction that he didn't know very much. It was during those four years, however, that he met my grandmother, Frances Smith.

FRANCES WAS BORN ON JULY 17, 1893, the first child of Newton Smith and Lottie McHuron. In 1886, Newton Smith moved to Baldwinsville, having accepted an offer from George Mercer to join the management team of Mercer Milling Company. Soon after his arrival, he began attending the First Baptist Church where he met Lottie McHuron, whom he married in 1888.

Lottie's family had been long-standing members of the First Baptist Church. Lottie's

Lester and Frances Flanders met at Michigan Agricultural College and were married on June 12, 1918.

After their wedding, Frances and Lester Flanders returned to Michigan; Lester gave up teaching to work on a farm owned by his brother Lewis.

Grandfather King, who himself had been baptized in the church at age 70, made sure his family attended services every Sunday. After church service, the children attended bible school while the men retired to the field outside, smoked pipes, and discussed farming issues. At times, the church services were divided into four parts. The first part was a children's sermon together with a children's choir; the second was for young people with a young person's choir; the third was for parents; and the fourth was for grandparents. On one Sunday evening, Lottie recalled, a male quartet sang an anthem "Ashamed of Jesus," and they sang it with so much feeling and pathos the minister said there wasn't any need for a sermon.

Baptisms took place in the river, generally in the early spring. On occasion, there would still be ice in the river that had to be moved out of the way with picks. After the immersion, those baptized were loaded onto carts and taken back to the church to get out of the wet clothes and then stand next to the stove to warm up.

Lottie was permitted to attend Saturday covenant meetings at 2:30 in the afternoon in a small upper room in the church, (which reminded Lottie "of the Upper Room in Jerusalem where the disciples met"), because the Saturday evening prayer meeting was held afterward. Lottie also recounted how a "Mrs. Crandall organized a missionary band for us, and they called us the Busy Bees, and, as I remember, we were supposed to sew for the heathen. I wonder what it possibly could have been that the heathen could use that I could sew at the time. Anyone in those days could wear a badge [which] was considered quite the thing. This is the one we had. I have kept it in my Bible for a bookmark."

Lottie also recalled how "we girls of the missionary band used to go on Sunday afternoons from 4 to 5 to read the Bible for her (a Mrs. Davis) because she couldn't see." With church services in the morning and at night, her entire Sunday was spent in one type of church activity or another.

This was the environment in which Grandma Flanders and her younger sisters, Winifred and Marjorie, spent the early years of their lives. Deeply devout and believing strongly in education, all three girls were required to study hard and to center their lives around the church. They lived at 26 Grove St., within walking distance to the mill and the school. After graduation from high school, Grandma Flanders decided to attend Michigan Agricultural College. She enrolled in the Home Economics Division. At MAC, she met Lester Flanders. They married on June 12, 1918 in Baldwinsville, and then returned to Michigan.

Dorothy Lou Flanders, taken when she was approximately two years of age.

Grandpa Flanders initially returned to teaching. He wrote: "The winter of 1917-1918, I had charge of the Agricultural Department of Decatur High School. It wasn't much of a department, and I didn't do much to improve it. My memory of that year is rather dim. I recall I had a class in solid geometry and I think a class in farm crops. Beyond these, I haven't the foggiest idea. I got $900 for nine months and was offered $1,000 for another year. However, St. Johns, twenty miles north of Lansing, offered $1,500 for twelve months so I signed up. In the meantime, Bro. Lewis had bought a farm near Battle Creek. In the spring of 1919, he came to St. Johns and asked me to help him on the farm. Not being too enthused with teaching school, I accepted. I spent one year on the farm with Lewis. One year in Decatur, one year in St. Johns, one year on the farm: one, two, three and out! Frances Smith of Baldwinsville and I had been married on June 12, 1918. Near the end of the year on the farm, Frances' father wrote that there was a vacancy at the Mercer Milling Co. We jumped at the chance to get off the farm. It had been a year of hard work, some minor frustrations, and no profit. On Aug. 9, 1920, I became one of the poorest salesmen that ever took to the road. However, it proved to be my last move—I stayed with the mill fifty-three

TOP *Lester Flanders'
father-in-law, Newton
Smith, was president
of the Mercer Milling
Company located
at 4 Syracuse St. in
Baldwinsville,
New York.*
BOTTOM *Flanders,
left, joined the Mercer
Company as a salesman
in 1920, at the invita-
tion of Smith, right.*

years. In 1912, the mill had been incorporated, and Dad Smith had been
made president. When he died in 1946, I succeeded him. In 1965, I sold
my interest (accumulated through the years) and stayed another six-and-
a-half years with the new boss."

Those early years of married life were years of challenge for Grandpa
Flanders. His first child, a daughter, died. After my mother, Dorothy, was
born, my grandparents lost twin sons. Then came the most crushing blow
of all. My grandmother contracted tuberculosis and passed on in May
1925. My mother was only three-and-a-half years old. In a letter to his
parents, Grandpa Flanders wrote:

*"Dear Pa & Ma:…Last Sunday she (his wife) seemed especially
bright and cheerful. At about 4 in the afternoon, Dorothy came
into her room to bid her goodbye as she was going down to her
grandmother's where she had been staying. They threw each other
kisses and went through the motions of hugging each other. After
Dorothy had gone, Frances urged me to go down to our organ*

recital at the church given by a blind man who has assisted in the Revival meetings... Dr. Geible had just finished singing the song of his own composition 'Someday We Will Understand' when word arrived for me to come home as quickly as possible. She was gone when I got there...

Before reaching her fourth birthday, Dorothy Lou Flanders suffered the loss of her mother, Frances, to tuberculosis in May 1925.

We have told Dorothy that her mother has gone to visit her little twin brothers and sister in Heaven, that God wanted her to come to help take care of the little children, and that we will go too someday if we are good. Dorothy thinks that is nice. After saying tonight 'I lay me down to sleep, etc.' she added, 'God bless Daddy, and Mother is up in heaven with the twins and Daddy wants me to be good.' That is a hard thing for her to be very alone at a time as she is certainly full of life. I've got a man-sized job ahead of me, and I pray I may be guided from above in instilling right principles in her mind. Tonight our minister called after prayer meeting and said that at the prayer meeting, they had voted unanimously to install a new 'Frances Smith Flanders Memorial Baptistry' in the church."

On June 27, 1928, Grandpa Flanders married Esther VanDenburg. In 1935, a son, Austin Lee Flanders (Lee), was born to them, but not before they shared the loss of another son. (My Uncle Lee, who is now in his 80s, married Margaret Olson (Peg) and were blessed with two children, Jonathan and Kristina, and five wonderful grandchildren.)

Grandpa Flanders faced yet another devastating loss when news arrived that his one surviving daughter had died in a plane crash in a foreign land, along with his grandson and son-in-law. The last time he had seen them was when they left Baldwinsville in November 1946. Yet Grandpa Flanders' trust in God never wavered. A week after the crash, he wrote the following to Dr. Fridell of the ABFMS: "So many things have happened in the past month that our minds have been in more or less of a daze. We hardly know whether or not we have thanked you for all that you have done in relaying news and expressing sympathy since Dorothy, Bob, and Teddy lost their lives in China. We do thank you and are very appreciative. In the weeks since, we have come to feel that the words 'lost their lives' are not the right ones to use. Truly, they have found their lives, for they have traversed two continents and a mighty ocean to reach 'the Gate of Heaven'. To me that has strange appeal. Dorothy had a wonderfully bright and ready smile, and it seems to me I can see it glorified and fairly sparkle as the gates of heaven opened wide for her and Teddy and so soon afterwards, for Bob. More and more I feel I have nothing to live for in the past but everything to live for in the future..."

PART III

MY PARENTS

Chapter 7

Robert Ades Vick

My father was born seven hours and twenty minutes short of Christmas day in 1917. His older sister, Ruth Arabelle, was born on November 1, 1915. As a toddler, my father could not pronounce her name and called her "Bubbles." The name stuck for the remainder of her life. Everyone in the family called her Bubbles. His younger sister, Ethel Carol, was born exactly five years after her sister. It wasn't until I was an adult that I learned her first name was Ethel, as she never used the name but went by her middle name, Carol.

The family grew up in the Thompson house at 142 Harvard St. This was the house in which Grandma Vick and her siblings were born and raised. Within walking distance of the house were located Rochester Elementary School #23, Monroe High School, and Immanuel Baptist Church. While all three of these institutions helped shape my father, it was the church that had the greatest influence on his life. My father was baptized at the age of nine, but it wasn't until attending camp at the age of 13 that his life was set on a path from which he never deviated. He wrote: "I had felt a message that I must tell others."

My father graduated from Monroe High School in 1936. His primary extracurricular activities, besides church, were playing in the orchestra and participating in the debate club. No matter what activity he engaged in, he did so with passion and focus. For instance, he was vehemently

LEFT *Robert Ades Vick was the middle child born to Clarence and Ethel Vick.*
RIGHT *The Vick children around 1930: Ethel Carol (who went by Carol) born November 1, 1920; older sister Ruth Arabelle (nicknamed "Bubbles") born November 1, 1915 and Robert, born December 24, 1917.*

opposed to the repeal of Prohibition. He wrote a letter on January 17, 1933 to Eleanor Roosevelt setting forth his disagreement with a speech she had made in support of repealing the 18th Amendment. Two weeks later he received a letter from her:

My dear Robert:

I have your letter of January seventeenth and I doubt very much if you really read my speech. I am therefore enclosing it. I am enclosing with my speech a statement from a Methodist minister in Kansas who seems to have had some of the same experience that I have.

As to the Eighteenth Amendment and what is to follow its repeal, I am just as anxious about as you are. Personally, I am a dry but there is no question in my mind that conditions as we have them today are bad and that fear of the future must not deter us from making a change.

I believe we are safer to go back to the old teaching of temperance in all things and to the responsibility of the individual for his own salvation, rather than to place all of our trust in the enforcement of a law which a majority of the people are not willing to have in force.

Very sincerely yours,
Eleanor Roosevelt (Mrs. Franklin D. Roosevelt)

The letter did not dissuade my father from continuing to speak out in support of Prohibition. An article appeared in the local newspaper announcing that my father, along with others, was to be a featured orator on the subject "Youth Faces the Liquor Problem."

During his high school years, my father had been appointed as a junior leader of a Boy Scout troop that met at Immanuel Baptist Church. A decision had apparently been made to deviate from the Scout handbook. In a letter to the Scout leader, he expressed his objection to such deviation by not adhering to strict standards for advancement. He wrote:

"I have had a vital interest in the troop as I was one of the possibly two who started it...It makes no difference to me of what the outcome of the scouting period of the boy's life is except that I would be proud to see them mature as scouting was planned...If you think it would be better to have just a boy's club consisting of dues and hikes and no national connection whatsoever, why don't you suggest it...I am willing to make a formal resignation of S. P. V. whenever you ask me...If by any case you wish me to continue, I will follow the handbook and not George Parker's wrong ideas of scouting. Your friend, Bob Vick."

After graduating from high school, my father matriculated at Denison University, an American Baptist institution, in Granville, Ohio, not far from Columbus. During his first semester, he joined Phi Delta

Theta fraternity and talked his way onto the marching band as a drum player (even though he had little experience playing the drums). By the end of his second year, he had taken on two pastorates in nearby towns, one with Kirkersville Baptist Church and the other with Fairfield Baptist Church in Thurston, while continuing with a full load of coursework. He also joined the

Robert Vick stands on the future site of Colgate Rochester Divinity School (CRDS) off Goodman Street in Rochester, New York, around 1926.

While attending Denison University in Granville, Ohio, Robert Vick took on two pastorates in nearby towns. He stands with his sisters, Ethel and Carol, in front of Fairfield Baptist Church in Thurston. RIGHT *He also served at Kirkersville Baptist Church.*

debate team and represented the college in regional competitions with other colleges and universities. During his senior year, he was elected to membership in Tau Kappa Alpha National Forensic Honorary Fraternity. Criteria for membership were at least two years of intercollegiate debating while maintaining a high scholastic rating.

Throughout my father's time at Denison, he was in constant contact with his parents, sharing his experiences and thoughts about sermons he was preparing or had given, and seeking advice. As he was finishing his ministry with the churches in Ohio, he was asked to deliver the baccalaureate sermon for the high school graduating class in Kirkersville. In describing the service he wrote to his parents:

> *"Well, the church was filled, and the S. S. (Sunday school) room doors flung back for the overflow. I gave that sermon all I possibly could. I certainly could feel God's power working then. My topic was 'Fellow graduates of 1940'…I developed it by saying that we are going to find four menacing facts—international breakdown, economic collapse, questioning of moral standards, and wide feeling of impotence of the church. All those have been in part made possible by Christian people. But God has given us young people at least four tools with which we can build a new world— intelligence, sense of humor, enthusiasm and the will to adventure, and Christ."*

My father's experiences pastoring the churches reaffirmed his conviction that God's call on his life was to become a pastor. In his "statement of call" submitted as part of his application to the American Baptist Foreign Mission Society to be commissioned as a missionary, he wrote:

"It was during my college days that I first thought seriously of foreign mission work. My senior year a commission was formed representing The World Fellowship interests of all student Christian groups in the state. I was made a co-chairman of the commission. We held a state convention at which some 200 students attended. The theme was the World Christian Community. That same year, under the impulse of the Amsterdam Youth Conference, the North American Christian Youth Conference was held in Toronto. It was at this conference that I began to feel the pull upon my heart that I must be a foreign missionary. One whole night after T. J. Koo had spoken, I did not sleep. But I tried to forget it. I had planned too long for the ministry in this country. Already I had been a student pastor for two years, and I liked the work immensely. In the spring of that year, I was invited to serve on the board of directors of the Student Volunteer Movement. My acceptance of this invitation, I believe, was God's way of making my decision crystalize. I became friends with missionaries and missionary enthusiasts of all denominations. In our retreats, and in our meetings, it became all the more clear to me that if I were to obey God's voice speaking within me, I must dedicate my life to foreign missions."

My father saw his college experience as preparatory to attending seminary. The question was where to attend. His first choice was Colgate Rochester Divinity School (CRDS) in his hometown. In another letter to his parents, my father shared his concern with attending a seminary where everyone knew him, along with his displeasure of a CRDS faculty member wanting to assign him to pastor a church in the small hamlet of Bushnell's Basin rather than in the larger community of Clifton Springs. He wrote in a letter concerning his quandary:

"Your letter about Bushnell's Basin is very confusing. It puts me on a spot. I don't particularly mind taking a 50% reduction in salary which this would mean as much as I hate to think of taking

a small church where all I can do or am expected to do is preach on Sunday. I'd rather not preach at all than do this. I want a laboratory where I can put into practice those principles I learn in the classroom. If I felt the chance of doing constructive work, I'd jump at the opportunity. Of course, I can't expect anything like I have out here. I asked for Clifton. Dr. Vickert doesn't believe Clifton is advisable for me. I'd like to know why!! At the same time, I hate to incur the wrath of Dr. Vickert who has been so kind, by intimating that I am dissatisfied with his efforts. When I came out here, neither the school nor the Baptist Convention advised me to go to Kirk and Thurston. I worked independent of the school. I'd like to do that in Rochester. Before causing any friction at that point, I'd go to Union (Theological Seminary) in a minute. It's hard for them to think of me other than the small child they knew me. Out here, I am the minister and am respected as such. I think I could handle Clifton as well as any. Why don't they give me a chance to candidate? There are plenty of fellows who need the preaching experience more than I."

In the end, Dr. Vickert won out. My father enrolled at CRDS for the fall semester of 1940 and took over as pastor of the community church in Bushnell's Basin. A fellow student at CRDS and close friend of my father was appointed associate pastor. During my father's two years at the

church, the Japanese attacked Pearl Harbor on December 7, 1941, and the United States entered World War II. In a letter to his congregation dated December 20, 1941, my father wrote:

The Vick family gathers in the backyard of their home at 142 Harvard St. around 1940. From left are Carol, Robert, Ruth Vick Happ, Ethel, and Clarence. Behind them is the shed that Frank Thompson and son George used for their paint and wallpaper business.

LEFT *Colgate Rochester Crozer Divinity School prior to the sale of its campus in 2019.* RIGHT *In his first two years attending divinity school, from 1940 to 1942, Robert Vick served as pastor of the Bushnell's Basin Community Church in a small hamlet near Rochester.*

"*Already there has begun to spread among our people great waves of cynicism and bitterness…It was hatred that inspired certain peoples of Europe and Asia to rise up against Democratic countries. The same hatred will cause their defeat…As a Minister of the Gospel of Love, and more particularly, as the only Minister in your Community, I have been doing much heart searching in regard to my responsibility to you…Especially in a time like this, you have the right to demand something from the church…I do not feel that I have any right to clutter my pulpit with a lot of pet theories concerning doctrines. I have the right to give you one thing. You have the right to expect one thing. Everything else must be secondary. I dedicate my pulpit to the giving to you of Jesus Christ, who is the ONE FOR THE SALVATION OF THE WORLD. As I send the Season's greeting to you—and I wish you all happiness, I also send this as my solemn and humble promise.*"

During my father's second year in seminary, he met my mother, Dorothy Lou Flanders, a nursing student at the University of Rochester. They were introduced to one another by another seminarian, Bob Bell. My mother wrote in a May 9, 1941 letter to her father:

Robert Ades Vick

"Last night I had a date with Bob Vick (Bob Bell's friend). We went over to his house for supper, then to a prayer meeting at his church and for a ride after. Have been out with him several times lately and have another date for Sunday afternoon. He is _very_ nice and I like him quite well. His father and mother are wonderful. I felt so much at home over there as if I had known them for a long time."

Chapter 8

Dorothy Lou Flanders Vick

My mother was born on October 7, 1921, about a year after her parents moved to Baldwinsville, New York, from Michigan. They took up residence at 15 McHarrie St., the home in which my mother was raised. As I noted earlier, when she was three-and-a-half, her mother died. She had already lost younger twin brothers and an older sister. Her mother's younger sister, Aunt Winn, stepped in to help take care of her, as well as her maternal grandparents, Newton and Lottie Smith, who lived close by at 26 Grove St. She was dedicated in the First Baptist Church, where her parents and grandparents attended, and later was baptized.

One of the few writings I have from my mother during those early years was a letter she wrote to her grandparents in Michigan. "Dear Grandma and Pa Flanders: How are you? This afternoon we were studying geography. This morning we wrote English. It was about a pumpkin. Mrs. Belknapp read it to us. I was one hundred in numbers work. And I was one hundred in spelling. I have been one hundred all the week so far. Daddy has a family of kittens. He had five of them but one of them ran away. And now he has four. Grandpa, Aunt Winn, and Grandma started for Maryland last Thursday morning. I would like to have you here now. Love you all from Dorothy Lou."

My mother's extended family was actively involved with her upbringing, especially as Grandpa Flanders had to make regular trips around central New York to take orders for flour. Even after Grandpa Flanders remarried approximately two years after his wife's death, 26 Grove St. was like a second home. There were periodic trips to Michigan to visit with her father's extended family as well as to other places around the country where his siblings and their children settled. The Flanders family was close-knit and saw each other as much as possible and stayed in regular communication. My mother was described as warm-hearted with a sunshine attitude and warm smile. She attended Baldwinsville Free Academy, graduating in 1939. She was deeply involved in church, and as she grew older, she taught younger children in Sunday school as well as summer vacation bible school.

My mother's desire to provide comfort and care to others led her to enroll in the nursing program at the University of Rochester in September 1939. In many ways, my mother leaving for college seemed to be harder for my grandfather than it was for my mother. In one of the first letters that Grandpa Flanders sent to my mother he wrote: "Things seem rather quiet around the house with you gone, altho you never made much noise. I look up and instead of seeing you across the dining room table, I have to look to see you looking at me from the top of the piano. Well, honey, is there anything you need? How about an extra blanket—have you needed it? And how about the heavy sweater? Let me know if there is anything at all, and I'll see that you have the wherewithal."

Soon after beginning her studies, my mother became involved in Baptist young adult groups. CRDS was located less than a mile from her nursing school. It did not take her long to begin to connect with students at the seminary. My mother was passionate about her faith and gravitated to others who shared that faith. By her second year, her social life inevitably involved one or more of the seminary students.

There was very little my mother did not share with her father, and including her social life. In a letter dated March 9, 1941, my mother wrote:

"It is Sunday morning, and Inez and I are sitting in the smoking room in our pajamas listening to the service at Central Presbyterian Church. In a few minutes, Lee Day, the fellow I went out with last night, will read the scripture. The circumstances under which I went out with him are a trifle out of order but it was

Dorothy Flanders and her father, Lester, kept in close touch via letters when she attended nursing school at the University of Rochester in the early 1940s.

exciting and loads of fun. About 8:15 last night, my buzzer rang and woke me up out of a sound sleep. He told me who it was, and that Bob Vick and Bob Bell had suggested that he take me out as he was in the mood to go roller skating and had called up everyone he knew. He wanted to meet me downtown as it was rather late, and he would have to go way down on the bus and back up to the dorm and would take too long. So I met him at 9:10, and we went roller skating. Gee, he is so nice and we had a wonderful time."

That letter brought an immediate response from Grandpa Flanders. He wrote:

"The sympathetic qualities that temper my thoughts make it difficult for me to answer your good letter in any but a considerate vein. To be called from a deep sleep in the night by a stranger

and at his invitation to travel across a big city to meet him on a street corner is a little beyond my experience. However, I am very much acquainted with my own weakness to do the thing I want to do in spite of the proprieties. So, I'm not going to scold. As your Grandfather Smith would say: 'If your foresight were as good as your hindsight, you might have handled the situation differently.' Had your mind not been cumbered with so recent a deep sleep, you could have said: 'Mr. D.! that certainly sounds exciting and I can't think of anything I rather do but your friends and my friends might think me quite forward since we haven't met. You bring Bob up some evening and then try again sometime for I do like to skate'…I have every confidence in my daughter. She will do the right thing when the doing is in her control. The thing to be careful about is to never allow oneself to get into a position where the control might pass into other hands…I often think of the things your Grandfather says. He told me once that he used to get pretty discouraged with himself because of mistakes he made. As he grew older, however, he learned not to take them to heart as he found it to be common with the human family in that way."

By letter dated March 16, my mother responded:

"I was very much surprised at the heading of your letter and its content last week, Daddy. I don't know whether I mentioned that on two occasions I had been introduced to Lee; however, it was a passing introduction and he didn't remember it at all. However, I agree now that you bring it up that it wasn't the thing to do, and I don't intend to do it again."

Two months later my mother wrote to her father. This was the first date between my mother and my father:

"Last night I had a very exciting date. Bob Bell's best friend called me up and asked me to go out. We went to an organ recital at Immanuel Baptist Church first, then for a ride until 12. We rode out to his church, which is a small country one about 20 miles from Rochester. He had preached there for nearly a year now. Good speaker, too. He is tall with light curly hair on the red side. We might go out again on my P. M. next week. He's going to read Tennyson to me. Isn't that exciting?"

There were times when my mother would experience a crisis of faith. In a letter she wrote to her father on June 19, 1941, she shared her confusion and misgivings. Her father wrote the following advice to her by letter dated June 25, 1941:

"Your letter of the 19th is before me and I note you are 'all mixed up'—well, lots of people are. However those who are most mixed up are the ones who let the things they cannot understand cloud their vision of the simple truths they can <u>feel</u> when they turn in simple faith to a loving Father who is always waiting with tender compassion for his children to take Him at His word. 'I will never leave thee nor forsake thee.' There are a great many books written, and many seem very sensible but if what they seem to teach is not compatible with this—LOVE—better not let them worry you too much. 'Now we see as through a glass darkly but then we shall know even as we are known.' "

In the fall of 1941, my parents decided to marry. Grandpa Flanders told me that my father—"to butter him up"—came to Baldwinsville and mowed his lawn. He then got up the courage to ask him for his daughter's hand in marriage. In a letter that Grandpa Flanders wrote to my mother that December, he stated:

"The letter Bob wrote makes me more willing than ever to place you in his care. I'm sure neither of you will ever regret the move you are making. Two, pulling together, can pull a much bigger load than two unwilling to cooperate one with the other. Always back each other up and boost and praise each other where praise is due. Don't make mountains of little faults. If Bob is late when you think he should be on time, instead of thinking of his lateness, think of the good you are sure he is doing to make him late. Meet him at the door with a smile always. Your mother always did that without fail. I am confident Bob is getting the best girl in Rochester. He thinks it now and will <u>know</u> it as the years come and go. You say you are young and can stand a lot. That is as it should be. However, I wish I could say this in letters a foot high! YOU CANNOT BE FAIR TO EACH OTHER, YOURSELVES, OR THE PUBLIC YOU SERVE IF YOU DO NOT SEE TO IT THAT YOU HAVE SUFFICIENT REST REGULARLY. Your own mother

*and I never dreamed she was overdoing but if she had not
been run down that deadly germ would never have gotten
the best of her. DON'T BE OUT NIGHT AFTER NIGHT
UNTIL MIDNIGHT—USE GOOD JUDGEMENT IN
PERSONAL CARE."*

For my mother, the period of engagement was not only one of deep-
ening her relationship with my father, but also with my father's family. In
a letter to her father dated February 11, 1942, my mother wrote:

*"I have just returned from the Seminary where I attended Dr.
Branton's class on Pauline letters. Today we took Paul's idea of
salvation as portrayed in Thessalonians. It was alive every minute,
and very, very interesting…Mr. Vick is taking the course. He
occasionally does take courses up there. He brought me back as
Bob had a class in Hebrew immediately following…Last night
Bob Bell with a date, Bob and I went tobogganing. What a thrill
we did have. We went down the Ellison Park run just once! And
I was in front without anybody to hide behind. There were quite
a few toboggans and I bet we went 50 miles per hour if we went a
mile. We all breathed a prayer as we were pushed over the top, I
guess…I stayed over at Bob's house all night, and he brought me
back at 11 a.m."*

Two days later Grandpa Flanders responded:

*"Your mother been worrying some for fear you were spending so
much time running around with Bob that you might be neglecting
your studying…I think, myself, once on Wednesday and a couple
of times over the weekend would be reasonable—you know Bob
has studies to take care of and exams to pass too. (Will your father
never get over offering advice?)…Your last letter sounded as if you
had recovered from that cranky spell. You are surrounded with
so much trouble it is no wonder you get 'down' once in a while.
One excellent remedy is to get regular rest. Anyone who gets all
tired out isn't fortified for the adversities. That's why I say you had
better have some definite ideas about the number of nights out per
week and the lateness of the hour. (There I go again—just can't
keep off the subject, can I?)."*

In spite of her father's admonishments, my mother wrote in a follow-up letter about a party she co-hosted and a ministry opportunity for my father:

"Last Friday was my day off, so Bob and I decided it would be a good time to do a little entertaining at his sister's house. We invited two couples, and there was Bubbles and Earl and us, which made eight. He took me out to Bubbles' house at 7:30 a.m. and I stayed all day helping her get ready. In the evening we played bridge, and who should drop in but Charlie Rose. You sent me a picture of that group, which was taken at our church back in 1936, Daddy, remember? He was president of the State Young Peoples Convention at the time... Sunday morning, we went to East Penfield Baptist Church where Bob preached. Really, I'm more enthusiastic about that proposition than ever. There were nearly 100 people out to church, and when Bob asked children to come up for the children's story, nearly twenty little ones under 8 years came up. They also have a junior church for them... From what I could see, they all enjoyed Bob's sermon very much. I wouldn't be surprised if he gets it. Wednesday night we both meet with the Pulpit Committee, and next Sunday, they will vote on it after the church service."

Two days later, my mother wrote:

"First of all I must tell you the good news. The church has called Bob, so it looks like East Penfield will be our home next year. We are so happy about it all because we both love the place already... We'll be able to start planning something definite at last. Bob thinks he will be going there June

Robert Vick served as pastor at East Penfield Baptist Church from 1942 to 1944.

Robert Vick and Dorothy Flanders in front of the nursing school at the University of Rochester prior to their wedding in 1942.

1st to preach and plans to stay out there during the summer. Gee, I've been walking on air all afternoon."

Later that spring, Grandpa Flanders wrote to my mother:

"Imagine you and Bob are both disappointed because you have to postpone the wedding. It was figuring a little too close. Better set the next date far enough ahead so it will be more sure. Now that you both are determined on the matter, the sooner after your time is completed, the better all things else being favorable. I want you to be happy, and I want it that way a great deal. I feel good when I see you smile and uneasy when I do not. Am thankful to say that makes me feel good most of the time. You are the apple of my eye, and you will not know how much that means until you have a child of your own."

Chapter 9

Preparation for Service

My parents were married at the Colgate Chapel located at Colgate Rochester Divinity School on September 19, 1942. About the wedding, my mother's brother, Lee Flanders, (who was fourteen years younger than my mother), wrote the following:

"The bride's family came the previous day, staying overnight at the parsonage. Besides myself this included my parents, also Grandpa and Granma Smith and Aunt Winn Smith, all from Baldwinsville. We all rode to the wedding in one car, our '41 Plymouth. After having gone only a short distance, Dorothy exclaimed 'Oh! I forgot my veil.' So we turned around and went back to get it. Prior to the date, the uncle of the groom, George Thompson, had apparently been hired to redecorate the house. (I think Bob and Dorothy were the first clergy family to occupy this parsonage)...I think the ladies of the church put on the reception. In those days it was customary for the bride and groom to slip away unnoticed. My father and I held a ladder to the front bedroom window at the right side of the house. This was out of view of the wedding guests. Dorothy put on a pair of pants and came down the ladder. Bob had the car waiting on the side of the road below the house. She cut behind the neighbor's house to join him."

Dorothy Flanders with her brother, Lee, at the family home at 15 McHarrie St. in Baldwinsville, New York.

A month later, on October 16, 1942, my mother graduated from the University of Rochester School of Nursing. My father still had his final year of divinity school to complete in addition to pastoring a growing congregation as well as periodically undertaking substitute teaching in the local high school. He finally graduated on May 19, 1943, and shortly thereafter was ordained in his home church, Immanuel Baptist.

My parents spent the three years following my father's graduation preparing to be commissioned as missionaries and heading to their mission assignment in China. My mother worked part time as a nurse, and my father continued to pastor the East Penfield Baptist Church community for another year. On January 2, 1944, my brother, Theodore ("Teddy") Flanders Vick, was born.

In March 1944, my parents, along with ten others, were appointed by the American Baptist Foreign Mission Society as Missionary-Appointees-in-Waiting with destination of China. They were commissioned on May 25, 1944 at the Northern Baptist Convention in Atlantic City. Because World War II was still raging, it was not possible for them to travel to their assignment.

Dorothy and Robert were married on September 19, 1942. They held their wedding reception at the parsonage of East Penfield Baptist Church, where Robert was pastor.

This gave my parents the time to learn the Chinese language, and my father the opportunity to be educated in agricultural matters. In the spring of 1945, he enrolled in courses at Cornell University's School of Agriculture in Ithaca to learn modern farming techniques that would provide him with the knowledge and skills needed to assist farmers in the remote area of Western China where my parents would live. The summer of 1945 my parents settled in Albion, about thirty-five miles west of Rochester, where my father led Sunday morning services at the First Baptist Church. I was born on September 30, 1945. I have been told that my father mistakenly announced from the pulpit that my brother had a new baby sister.

The American Baptist Foreign Mission Society (ABFMS) was founded in 1814 and is now called International Ministries. This logo was in use at the time of the Vicks' commissioning as missionaries to China.

During the spring of 1946, my parents moved to Cheshire, Connecticut, and enrolled in an intensive language program at the Institute of Chinese Studies at Yale University. After completion of language school, my parents were formally commissioned as missionaries during a service at the First Baptist Church of Summit, New Jersey, on June 16, 1946.

For the next few months, while waiting to be transported to China, my parents traveled to different churches around New York, Ohio, and New England, sharing their call to the mission field. They spoke at different church conferences and camps. My father's Christian camping experience had played an enormous role in nurturing his faith journey, and he used every opportunity to share his faith with young people during summer camping programs.

During a sermon my father preached at Lincoln Baptist Church not far from Rochester, he shared the following experience:

> *"A few weeks ago I stood on the top of a hill a mile or two outside the little town where my college is situated. It was early evening but the sun hadn't quite set. The big red ball of fire was becoming redder and redder as it neared the horizon. In the valley below,*

NEW MISSIONARIES

Presented to the Northern Baptist Convention Atlantic City, N. J.

Further information about these missionaries is presented in a little pamphlet called "NEW MISSIONARIES," to be distributed by the ushers at the Commissioning Service fo rMissionaries.

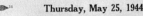

Thursday, May 25, 1944

REVEREND PHYLLIS RENNER, W.A.B.F.M.S., has recently relinquished her service to two churches in London, New Hampshire, in order to take an intensive course in French preparatory to sailing to the Belgian Congo to do evangelistic work among women and children. She is attending the Berlitz School of Languages in Boston.

MISS EVELYN WALLACE, W.A.B.F.M.S., is continuing courses in Public Health preparatory to going to South India to train Telugu nurses to minister in rural and urban areas. Since India is largely a nation of villages, Miss Wallace's experience in this country as a rural missionary will further fit her for her task.

DR. MARY KIRBY, W.A.B.F.M.S., has completed her internship and is ready to return to Assam, the land of her birth. Her early life in the field there will make unnecessary the usual period of orientation for new missionaries. Her parents, Dr. and Mrs. Herbert W. Kirby, now head the leper work in Jorhat.

MISS DORIS M. WISEMAN, W.A.B.F.M.S., is the twin sister of Miss Dorothy M. Wiseman, R.N., presented at the last convention. Miss Wiseman has finished her final study in the Africa Department, Kennedy School of Missions, and is prepared to undertake educational work in the Congo.

REV. CHESTER J. JUMP, JR., A.B.F.M.S., pastor of the Hilda L. Free Largier Parish, London Center, Vermont, is a new appointee with Belgian Congo as his destination. While carrying on his studies at Colombia University and Union Theological Seminary he served as Day's Worker, Baptist Tabernacle, New York.

MRS. MARGARET SAVIDGE JUMP, A.B.F.M.S., with a rich background of experience as teacher in Williamstown High School, Pa., is secretary work in New York City, and a member of the faculty of London Institute, will go to Belgian Congo as missionary. While working time to sail the people will prepare themselves more fully for work in Africa.

REV. HERBERT M. RANDALL, A.B.F.M.S., a student pastor at the Jaynelee Baptist Church, Chicago, will serve in Assam. His training at Gordon College and Northern Baptist Seminary has fitted him for missionary service. He, like others, will go where need is greatest.

MRS. EDNA ANDERSON RANDALL, A.B.F.M.S., also has accepted the call of God to serve on mission fields. She is a graduate of Moody Bible Institute and of Northern Baptist Theological Seminary. Her five years of service in this country will be excellent background for phases of mission work.

REV. ROBERT A. VICK, A.B.F.M.S., is designated to China. His experience in pastoral work, both in Rochester and Fairport, New York, will serve him well. He is a graduate of Denison University and of Colgate-Rochester Divinity School.

MRS. DOROTHY FLANDERS VICK, A.B.F.M.S., a graduate nurse, has received excellent training at the University of Rochester School of Nursing, and through the Extension Department of Colgate-Rochester China will welcome her as a true follower of the Great Physician.

DR. GEORGE E. HALE, A.B.F.M.S., graduate of William Jewell College, Southern Baptist Theological Seminary and the Harvard Medical School, is resident physician at Pennsylvania Hospital, Philadelphia. Medical missionaries are greatly needed on every field. His destination will be determined by the greatest need, when opportunity opens for sailing.

MRS. MARY PARKER HALE, A.B.F.M.S., of Baton Rouge, Louisiana, is a graduate of Louisiana State College, with M.A. from the State University. With editorial experience with the American Baptist Publication Society Mrs. Hale combines her specialized work. Both Dr. and Mrs. Hale have indicated their willingness to serve wherever designated.

REV. EUGENE R. ABBOTT, A.B.F.M.S., pastor of the Cherryville Baptist Church, New Jersey, has just received appointment to evangelistic work in the Belgian Congo field. Mr. Abbott is a graduate of Miami University, Oxford, Ohio, and of Crozer Theological Seminary. Specialized study at the Kennedy School of Missions will aid training of native.

MRS. VIVIAN WHIPPLE ABBOTT, A.B.F.M.S., will find ample scope for her nurses' training and experience in Belgian Congo. She, too, took work at Crozer Seminary. A native of Ohio, wife of a Baptist minister, she hopes to sail for Congo when opportunity opens.

REV. WILLIAM W. SUTTERLIN, A.B.F.M.S., of Arizona and California, has offered himself for evangelistic work in China. In the Japanese Relocation Center in Hunt, Idaho, in 1943 Mr. Sutterlin gave varied service. A 1944 graduate of the Berkeley Baptist Divinity School, with a B.A. from the University of Redlands, he is trained for effective service.

MRS. RUTH HARVEY SUTTERLIN, A.B.F.M.S., of Portland, Oregon, is a graduate of Linfield College, with a Master's degree from Berkeley Baptist Divinity School. She has been in youth and group work with migrant children and has had experience at Northern California's Christian Friendliness Missionary. Mr. and Mrs. Sutterlin will attend the School of Chinese Studies in California.

WORLD EMERGENCY APPOINTMENTS:

In addition to the missionaries listed on these pages, there have been nine appointments made through the World Emergency Forward Fund. These missionaries are working under the joint supervision of the two Home Mission Societies. They are stationed in crowded defense areas in various parts of this country where they are helping to solve the problems of defense workers and their families. These appointees and their locations are as follows:

Miss Hilda Dolores Buck, Springfield, Vermont; Miss Eva Dahljelm, Vancouver, Washington; Miss Josephine Ellen Hagman, Portland, Oregon; Mrs. Minnie Esterro Jackson, Richmond, California; Miss Marie I. Johnson, Vallejo, California; Miss Allison Osborn, Bridgeport, Connecticut; Miss Florence F. Porter, Portland, Oregon; and Mrs. Ruth Ellen Van Dyke, Wheeling, West Virginia.

Robert and Dorothy Vick (second row from bottom) were commissioned as missionaries bound for China in May 1944. Also listed are William and Judy Sutterlin (bottom right), who also served in China, and Chester and Margaret Jump (above the Vicks). Chester Jump eventually became executive director of ABFMS and served in several roles, primarily in the mission field in what is now known as the Democratic Republic of the Congo.

the toilers of the soil were finishing their tasks, weary with fatigue and seeking rest in the tranquil hour of twilight. I could hear the bells in the town of our chapel pealing out the strains of the beloved hymn, 'Nearer, my God, to Thee, nearer to thee.' The sun had about slipped out of view when very softly one could hear a bugle playing taps. 'Day is done. Gone from the sun, from the lakes, from the hills, from the sky. All is well. Safely rest. God is nigh.' That moment, I felt a strange nearness to God. He seemed to demand my life; my all."

Robert Vick leads a Bible study at a conference in the mid-1940s.

Chapter 10

The Journey to Shanghai

The summer of 1946 was one of great anticipation for my family. In early July, my parents learned that the four of us would be sailing on the *S.S. Marine Lynx* from San Francisco to Shanghai as early as August 23rd. The home office of the American Baptist Foreign Mission Society in New York City sent letters regarding documentation needed and recommended items to pack. The wife of a classmate of my father at CRDS who had also been commissioned to serve in China wrote that they had been notified of the August sailing date and were very much looking forward to traveling together. Then on July 26, my parents received a letter stating that space aboard the ship assigned to ABFMS missionaries had been greatly reduced, and priority was being given to older missionaries returning to the field. As a consequence, there would be no room for my family.

My father and mother were extremely disappointed, but they saw this delay as an opportunity to continue sharing their mission vision with the American Baptist family. My father's CRDS classmate and his wife, Gordon and Jean Gilbert, had secured passage on the ship and arrived in China in October. They then traveled to their mission station in Hangchow, where Dr. Gus Naismith and his wife, who also had a connection to CRDS, had established a hospital and started the Wayland Academy. Their arrival only increased my parents' sense of urgency to get to China as quickly as possible.

Soon they were notified that they would leave from San Francisco on the same *Marine Lynx* after it returned from China, most likely on December 1. They had completed much of their preparation during the summer, including sending household belongings to San Francisco, where they would be loaded on their ship to China. Their friends Herb and Mary Jackson, who were serving as missionaries at the Andhra Christian College in Guntur, South India, wrote to them of the widespread violence all over India, and the killing of thousands in areas where ABFMS had mission stations. They wrote: "We suppose you will find a great deal of unrest in China, along with many dangers and problems. We would like to hear about conditions there, and especially the attitude toward white people as such and toward missionaries as such. It is my understanding that China went through a period of hating the West, the white man, and missionaries, but that that day has gone, and all three of the above-mentioned are accepted with open arms. Still I expect communistic influence has done much recently to create aversion to the West and to Christianity."

In early November, my parents, my brother, myself, and my father's parents loaded a small trailer with remaining personal items. We piled into Sarnia (the name given to the car) and started on the journey to San Francisco. A hammock was somehow slung for me. My parents planned the route around visiting as many relatives and friends as possible.

The trip to San Francisco was chronicled by mother through frequent letters to her father. Following are extracts from those letters she mailed upon reaching San Francisco:

December 2, 1946

Having finally made it to San Francisco the day before, on December 2, my family went to Pier 44 to see off the General Maigs, *which was to leave carrying missionaries to China, a few of whom they knew. My mother wrote: "Passengers were given different colored streamers, and they would take one end and toss the roll to someone on the pier who would take the other end. It was a pretty sight to see all the different colored streamers extending from the ship to the pier. One Chinese mother holding a child a little older than Paul tossed one to us and motioned for Paul to take it. The two babies, one Chinese and one American, both held an end, and it represented a gesture of friendship which was rather*

76

Ethel Vick, left, and Dorothy Vick, along with Paul and Teddy, are ready for the drive to California in November 1946.

ABOVE *Robert Vick with Ethel, Dorothy, Teddy, and Paul stop to enjoy the view on the trip.* LEFT *Teddy, right, looks up at the inscription of the Builder's Creed etched on a massive stone tablet at the entrance to the Great Mausoleum at Forest Lawn Memorial Park in Glendale, California. Dr. Hubert L. Eaton, founder of Forest Lawn, wrote the Builder's Creed, which begins with the words "I Believe in a Happy Eternal Life."*

Dorothy Vick with Teddy, left, and Paul on the trip to San Francisco. Dorothy often wrote letters to her father during the trip and their stay in San Francisco.

symbolic…Sunday is a big meeting at Oakland Auditorium for 900 missionaries who are to sail on the Lynx and Marine Falcon, which is to sail a few days later. There are 700 missionaries to go on our boat. This is more than the first sailing. They say conditions will be pretty rugged but we can take it providing we get enough sleep and good food. Daddy, you were worrying about our staying up late nights but you didn't have to…The children are thriving on this life. They've been remarkably good, have slept well in the car, and gotten to bed in good season every night."

December 7, 1946

"Dec. 7, 1946 and the anniversary of Pearl Harbor. We thought those war years would never end but they have and we can pray that they never occur again…Last night Bob and I with Tracy Gibson who used to be at Lincoln near E. Penfield and at CRDS went up on the Berkeley Hills where we could see for miles and miles. It was a very clear night, and we could see a city forty-five miles down the coast. Beautiful night…Yesterday we took the children to the zoo with Joe Esther's family. He is Dutch Reformed and is going on the Lynx too. We met them at Cornell."

Flyer announcing a Missionary Rally to be held in the Oakland Auditorium.

On December 16, 1946, about 700 missionaries including the Vicks set sail from San Francisco bound for China on the S.S. Marine Lynx, a converted troop ship that had made the voyage previously.

December 10, 1946

"We had a visitor up to our room. Dr. Criswell from W. China, who is a Baptist and is also sailing on the Lynx. She is a very lovely, cultured woman and we talked for three hours before she left. Think we shall enjoy being in the same station as her...Last Sunday there was staged in the Oakland Auditorium, a huge building seating about 5,000 persons, a bon voyage meeting for the missionaries who are to sail within the next two weeks. There are 980 missionaries going, which is the largest group ever to leave the shores of the U.S. at one time. About 280 of them are going on a boat other than ours. Approximately 400 were present to march in the processional down the center isle of the auditorium. The others hadn't arrived yet as it was a week early. Dr. C. Oscar Johnson of St. Louis, a Baptist, gave the address, and it was a very inspiring affair...Dad and mother Vick left this AM. There were no tears, at least visible ones. Mother V. said the meeting Sun. and Dr. Johnson's talk helped to ease the strain and dread. Wish you could have been there too. I saw a man up in the balcony that reminded me of you, Dad, so I made believe it was you. It was almost as good as having you there."

ABOVE *Waving to a large crowd of well-wishers prior to leaving the dock are at left, Robert holding Paul and Dorothy holding Teddy.* RIGHT *Dorothy, Robert, and Teddy on the ship's deck.*

December 15, 1946

"It's rather a solemn thought when one gets to the point of actually leaving the good old U. S. I can appreciate what a tremendous psychological adjustment it must have meant for all the soldiers and sailors. After all, they were going out to enemies, and we're going out to friends…Here we are on the boat standing in line for dinner…Boy, oh boy! Wish you could see this jumble. There is a huge room where I am located with the children. The bunks are three deep. It seemed that nearly everyone was on when we came, and at first, I thought I would have to put the children on one end of the room and me at another but Dr. Criswell found *me two together so we are all set. It finally developed that I have four berths together. Can use one or two for baggage racks. There is little space between rows and lots of screaming children... We're at the table now. Serve cafeteria style. We have a big serving of chicken, potato, rice, peas, dressing, and pumpkin pie. It may be the last meal we'll enjoy but we're fortified with some Mothersill's Seasick pills so here's hoping... Met a Chinese army officer at the hotel this a.m. who is also going on the Lynx. He said that Chengdu is a wonderful place, very quiet, etc. Said the climate is excellent, and there is lots of food.... At 2:30 p.m. we were on deck having our pictures taken for the Crusader... We were glad our parents weren't there in one way, as the leave-taking would have been much more difficult. It was exactly 4:35 p.m. when we felt the boat begin to move, and the space between us and the pier began to widen. The streamers of many colors that stretched from deck to pier broke as the distance grew greater. There was a large crowd to see the boat leave, and everyone was shouting and waiving. I lost a couple of little tears as I thought of not seeing the U.S. again for six years but soon noticed that no one else was that sentimental... We passed under the Bay Bridge over which we had driven many times when Dad and Mother Vick were still with us. Also passed very close to Alcatraz Island. The day had been rather cloudy but as we approached the Golden Gate Bridge, there was one of the loveliest sunsets I have ever seen. Stood and watched the lights of the city for a long time. Thought of all the many people who had seen America for the first time and what dreams and hopes many of them had... It wasn't long before the loud speaker announced supper... Meals are served cafeteria style. Food is put on a sectional tray. The only dishes are cups and soup bowls. The only spoons are the size of table spoons. Paul's mouth stretches a little bigger with each bite. I wish you could see our hatch. I am in hatch #6 with approximately 136 others. Cots are suspended by chains. They are three deep in the women's quarters and two deep in the men's... There are 250 children on board under 16 years of age and half of them are in #6. We all have a howling good time. One good feature is the engine room is next door and the noise from that drowns out the crying and squalling."*

December 16, 1946

"About 3 a.m. Monday morning I awoke. The boat was rolling
from side to side. Very frequently it would give a big heave, and
someone's baggage would come crashing down. Two or three poor
ladies were retching, and others were hurrying by with their hands
over their mouths in the direction of the bathroom. Some made it,
others didn't. I was scared for a time. It sounded like a bad storm
outside. Could hear the waves breaking over the bow of the boat, or
so I thought. I'd rather sink in the daytime than at night. However,
my skepticism soon passed. Jumped out of bed and ate an orange
as someone had advised as a guard against seasickness. But it
wasn't long before my orange came back, whence it started in small
doses at fifteen-minute intervals. Everyone else was sick too, so the
steward had the pleasant task of running up and down the aisles
bringing cans and carrying them out. By 9 o'clock I hadn't seen
anything of Bob, who I presumed was having troubles of his own,
so with basin under my arm I staggered up to the dining room
with the children. They were as lively as ever. I managed to feed
them a little before the elements overcame me, and I rushed out
to use the basin. The rest of the morning passed in much the same
manner with everyone around moaning and groaning and feeling
quite miserable. Around noon time Bob came down looking rather
white and shaky…Bob has an extra berth next to him so we moved
Teddy over there, which has been a big help to me."

December 17, 1946

"Bedlam breaks loose at 6 a.m. with the waking of all the babies.
Got up wondering if there was to be a repeat performance of
Monday, but Bob and I both felt good so guess we acquired our
sea legs… The children have been organized into groups for play
in the morning, which is nice for them and relieves the mothers
for a while. The top deck, called the sun deck, is used for Teddy's
age group. The railings are lined with canvas so it is a safe place to
play. Teddy goes at 9 a.m. He loves it and seems to get along quite
well with the rest… The ship wasn't built for civilian travel obvi-
ously. There are only two bars for railings and children could easily
slip under the bottom one and hence overboard. In fact, Teddy

gave us a scare on Mon. He threw a paper bag over the railing and because it didn't quite go over the ledge, he started to go under the railing to push it over. We called to him quickly, and I think he sensed the danger because he came right back. We haven't let him loose since then."

December 27, 1946

"Have been getting very lazy so have been neglecting adding on news each day...Christmas was fun even though it didn't seem like the Christmas we've been used to...Tuesday, the day before Christmas, there were parties for all the children. The ones of Teddy's age had theirs in the morning. I was on the committee. They sang some carols and played some games. Then Santa came. Had a real Santa. The churches of S.F. had taken the names of all the children, so there was a gift for nearly everyone. Had a Christmas tree, gaily decorated. Teddy got three picture books. Paul was overlooked but he had a grand time watching all the rest, especially Santa. Mother Vick bought us a creche of the manger scene, and Bob and I put that up by the Christmas tree and inserted a light from the tree in the stable roof so it cast a soft red glow on the scene within...Christmas Eve, Teddy and Paul hung up their stockings on the side of their bunks. I bought two net stockings in S.F. filled with candy, gum, nuts, and a little boat, which they found hanging there in the a.m. Then after breakfast we opened the few gifts we had put in our hand luggage. Bob gave me a pretty red sweater. I gave him a gold bracelet for his watch. Teddy has a little tea set and Paul a top."

December 29, 1946

"Yesterday we had our first glimpse of land. It was just a piece of rock sticking up out of the ocean. It was supposed to be the southern tip of the Islands of Japan...Most of the children cough and have colds. It is terribly drafty all over the boat. Teddy and Paul both have them too. Teddy coughed so much yesterday he couldn't keep anything in his stomach, and we kept him in bed all day...Paul just has a perpetual runny nose but feels pretty good."

Chapter 11

A Month in China

After years of preparation for missionary work and more than two weeks at sea, my parents arrived in Shanghai with Teddy and me in tow. My mother wrote in great detail about their arrival and settling in:

"Greetings and salutations from Shanghai, China! What a joy it is to be here. The last two days on the ship were pretty trying...Teddy had a bad cold and developed a high fever...Paul has the sniffles too but has nothing serious. He is riding around in the Taylor tot here in our living, dining room while I'm writing this. Teddy is sleeping soundly. To start from the beginning, our first glimpse of China was about 8 a.m. Tuesday. As we came on deck after breakfast, we were traveling up the Huangpu River. On both sides we saw low, flat countryside with green fields...There were many small fishing boats at the mouth of the river with their big oriental sails...As we went further up the river the sampans and junks began to appear. The sampans are the small house boats on which families live, and the junks are large cargo boats. The sampans and the people on them were interesting. The man would stand at the stern and hold a long paddle, which was used to steer the boat. The woman would stand a few feet from him pulling back

LEFT *The* S.S. Marine Lynx *sailed on the Huangpu River into Shanghai.* BELOW *Passengers disembarked from the ship onto this pier on December 30, 1946.*

and forth on a rope, which must have been some kind of propeller in the bottom to keep the boat going. In many of them were two or three children sitting watching our ship...The only shelter was a rounded tunnel open at both ends in the center of the boat...One sampan came very close to the ship. We waved and smiled at the woman tugging at the propeller rope, and she smiled back. There were two little children, a boy and a girl, and we held Paul up and waved his hand. They all laughed....Going through customs was an ordeal we all dreaded...We passed alphabetically along a line to have our passports examined. Then an officer was assigned to examine our baggage...all of this started around 11 a.m. but it was 2:30 p.m. when we walked down the gang plank and felt our feet on terra firma again…Bob Taylor, our mission treasurer, was there to meet us with a car. We were taken to a Methodist building called the Blackstone Apartments…We are in a dormitory. Teddy, Paul, and I are in a room with thirteen beds (camp cots but comfort-able)…Bob is staying across the hall with about as many men…The men and women can eat together at least. I will be so glad when we can be a family again…Clarence Vickert and Connie sailed on the General Meigs for home yesterday…They are the ones who are members of Immanuel Church in Rochester and have been long overdue for their furlough…At any rate, Bob leased their summer cottage for us for the next two summers up in the hills…"

During their stay in Shanghai in January 1947, the Vick family lived at the Blackstone Apartments, a building owned by the Methodists. Photo taken in 2011 on a trip to China made by Paul and Joyce Vick and Ben Chan.

"Connie Vickert and I took the children to the barber shop…I took Teddy and carried Paul down….The Chinese girls in the barber shop were crazy about Paul. They walked him up and down and entertained him royally. Even dressed him up again when we were ready to go. Connie said the Chinese love foreign children and especially redheads…Yesterday I walked over to the American School…there are many lovely buildings but they are empty shells or rather were when the Japanese moved out….Children from 11 yrs. up through high school are boarded but they take day stu-dents for both primary and high school years. We looked into the laundry where the Japanese had tortured their victims for infor-mation and then shot them. The floor had been covered with blood stains after the war. It was terrible feeling to walk where they had walked and think of what had happened only a short time before."

My father wrote to his family:

"We are not sure just when we shall leave Shanghai. We do have reservations on a China National Air Command (CNAC) plane for the 21st. This would take us to Chungking. Then we would have to dicker for another to Chengdu… The alternative is the Lutheran Plane (owned by the Lutherans) which would take us directly to Chengdu on the 15th. The only stickler is that this would cost four times as much as the other. We must still wait and see whether or not the Board will give its O.K. to this. When finally we do arrive in Chengdu, we shall be living with the Grahams. At least we shall be getting our meals there. We might live in a house by ourselves nearby, or we might have a couple of rooms in their house… We are now anxious for up-to-date news from home. Where did you spend Christmas? What gifts did everyone get?…How is Uncle George? We have thought about you, Uncle George, many times, and hope you are really taking care of yourself now. (My father then inquires about his sisters' children.) I'll bet you saw a difference in Randall, and even in Sharon during the six weeks you were gone. Perhaps even Bobby shows some differences. We wish—how we wish it sometimes!—that we could

Robert and Dorothy Vick and children worshipped at the Community Church in Shanghai in 1947 while they waited for the opportunity to fly to western China. Photo taken in 2011.

*drop in for a surprise "hello" sometime... But we are headed for
a very important work, and we know we have your prayers and
constant concern."*

By letter to her parents dated January 16, 1947, while staying in
Hangchow with the Gilberts, my mother wrote:

*"How our hearts yearn for these people even though we have been
here such a short time. They need so much, and we have so much
we can give them in the way of gaining new hope when the way
is open. The first barrier is the language, and we're practically
tearing our hair at being forced to stay here when we want so
much to reach Chengdu and begin our language study. Right now
we think we may be leaving on the Lutheran Plane, January 23rd.
However, January 22nd is the Chinese New Year celebration, and
business drops to a standstill for a week or so then... We're leaving
for Shanghai tomorrow and hope to be in Chengdu by the time
you receive this."*

After returning to Shanghai, by letter dated January 22nd, my father
wrote to friends:

*"Everything has militated against good morale. The initial dis-
appointment was, of course, the three years of waiting before we
finally did sail. Then the trip under hard circumstances. Arriving
in Shanghai, we were taken to a hostel where we are sleeping on
army cots in separate dormitories. We eat in a common dining
room, but there is no privacy whatsoever... Our delay here is
caused by a chain of circumstances. We were scheduled to leave
for Chengdu by plane on the 15th. That week all planes were
grounded because of so many crashes here. Then, last Monday
we were all slated to leave on the Lutheran plane, which we had
chartered to Chengdu. Two things prevented our going. Paul came
down with the chickenpox, and our plane made a forced landing
near Peking, which means it is grounded indefinitely. SO HERE
WE SIT!!"*

While in Shanghai, my mother learned of the death of her grandfather Smith. In a letter to her Grandmother Smith and Aunt Winn, my
mother wrote:

1331 Rue Lafayette
Shanghai, China
22 January 1947

Dear Bob and Beth: *Bell*

Perhaps, by the time this letter arrives we should be greeting yet another Bell. It is now four months since we last saw you, and if my memory serves me rightly, this month or next ought to mark a very important milestone in your life together. We are quite anxious to hear all about it.

Our ship, the Marine Lynx--commonly known by its passengers as the Marine Jynx--sailed out of S. F. on the 15th of December. We travelled steerage, and we would like to forget all about it. About four hundred women and children were packed together in the same hatch. Just last Sunday Paul came down with the chicken pox which he caught on the ship. A child down stairs has the mumps, so probably ours will begin swelling soon. The kids proved good sailors and mommy and daddy only had one woozy day, so it could have been worse. On the 31st, we arrived in Shanghai--already for a long stay here.

The difficulty has been in getting plane passage to Chengtu. We were all set to go more than a week ago when all planes in China were grounded for a week because of so many recent crashes. Then, we had a reservation on a chartered plane owned by the Lutherans to go this past Monday. Two things prevented. Paul came down with the chicken pox on Sunday and the plane had made a forced landing near Peking last week and so was indefinitely grounded. SO HERE WE SIT.

Our impressions of China could, and I presume, will be better. We had sun for the first three days. Since then we have had almost constant rain and damp and cold. We are staying at a hostel, sleeping on army cots in separate dormitories, eating not much more than basic rations, and paying $90,000 or $30.00 U. S. a day for the privilege. We had one bright spot, however, when last week we took the train to Hangchow and stayed with the Gilberts for almost a week. They have their own home on the Wayland Academy Compound, have their own servants, a good sized garden, and are already doing some mission work besides studying the language. We had a great time there visiting. One day we went hunting. Although we only shot two pheasants (I didn't wing either), we did see a lot of the country and especially the farmers and the life they live.

We haven't seen too many outward evidences of the war. Oh, there are pillboxes everywhere and we have seen a few buildings that had been bombed. There is a lot of evidence of misused and run down buildings etc. One of the most striking cases of this is the Hangchow University where the buildings had been completely stripped of everything, windows broken etc. The lovely organ was reduced to a few pieces of wood strewn around.

Hangchow is noted for its great Buddhist Temple. In this Temple there are three large statues of Buddha at least fifty feet high. There are at least fifty smaller statues about twelve feet high--all in gold. This was quite a sight to behold.

One interesting sight in China is to see the many graves all along the countryside. The coffins are put on top of the ground and covered with straw --then dirt. Each year dirt is added. This sort of gives veneration, I suppose. You ought to come over here and crusade for cremation, Beth.

Please write us bringing us up to date on news of common interest. Simply address our letters to W. China,Union Univ. in Chengtu, Sze, China. I am enclosing this letter with a letter I'm sending home. They will remail it. It cost $950 to send 5 grams by air to the states.

If congratulations are in order, be assured of double from all of us.

Love,
Bob, Dot, Teddy, Paul

Robert Vick chronicled his family's first few weeks in China in this letter to friends Bob and Beth Bell.

"How strange it seems not to be including Grandpa in this too. Our hearts do ache for you knowing that you must be going through your Gethsemane. What a blessed hope we have as Christians that death is not the end but just a door into another room that is bigger and brighter. I really never thought when we parted last summer that it would be the last time we would see Grandpa here. I'll never forget the wonderful times we all used to have together on Grove Street. Your home was a haven of refuge for me while I was growing up, and I'll never, never forget all the pleasant memories. I think I always looked forward to Sundays as the best day in the week. I can see you, Grandma, and see Grandpa in church on Sunday and coming up afterward to say, 'Going home to dinner with us, Dorothy Lou?' Then I'd run and ask Dad, and most of the time he'd say 'yes'. Then after dinner we'd go off to North Syracuse or over to Heids for a hot dog or down to the mission. They were always wonderful Sundays. Then there were the summer times we'd go on picnics and Skaneateles Lake to Camp.... You used to read Grace Livingston Hill books with me and I felt I could talk about anything that came into my head, and you would be interested. It is all these things that make people live on forever regardless of whether their early shell is here on earth or not."

Word finally arrived that the long-awaited flight would be leaving Shanghai on January 28, 1947.

Chapter 12

The Worth of a Life

*"The worth of a life is not to be measured by its length
but by the warmth of its devotion and the quality
of its service to a great cause."*

T hat inspirational quote, unattributed, is one of several quotations
and scripture references in a booklet produced as a memorial to
my parents and published by the American Baptist Society. On
the cover is the title *The Worth of a Life* in English with the same written
in Chinese characters.

Inside the booklet, the young adult faces of my parents peer out in
formal head shots. There's also a photo of the four of us; my mother holds
me, about nine months old. She is smiling broadly, as she often did in
photos, as she stands next to my father. My father wears a more serious
expression as he was also wont to do. Teddy stands in front of him, and
my father's long left arm reaches down to hold Teddy's hand. The photograph was taken at summer camp in 1946.

My parents and Teddy were buried in Hankow on Monday, February
3, 1947 in what the booklet called "a lovely service."

*"Everything was done reverently and unhurriedly as though in
a cathedral, and through the service I know that God spoke to
one troubled soul. Afterward I heard that more than one had this*

experience. My burden of horror was lifted. The festering, unanswerable 'Why?' fell back before the assurance that even out of this evil, God can bring some good to His church—in China and Canada and the United States. I, too, felt the triumph when the challenge rang out, 'Oh death, where is thy sting? Oh grave, where is thy victory?'"

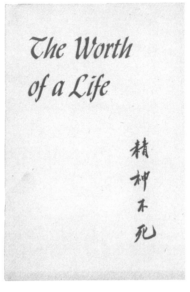

The Worth of a Life

精
神
不
死

The American Baptist Society published this booklet as a memorial to Robert, Dorothy, and Teddy Vick; it includes excerpts from memorial services.

Those were the words of Eunice Peters, writing specially concerning the death of her friend Beatrice Kitchen.

My parents were also remembered in a sermon given by Pastor T.E. Tsiang on February 2, 1947 in Shaohing Baptist Church in China. Tsiang had attended CRDS for one year, and he met my parents while we were visiting the Gilberts in Hangchow. Tsiang wanted my father to visit his church prior to us leaving Shanghai, but there hadn't been time.

Tsiang titled his sermon "How the Death of the Vicks Impressed Me as a Christian." He explained to his congregation of several hundred people how he had met my parents.

> "They came to China to help people to know Jesus Christ. I admired their spirit but I as well as their friends felt very, very sorry to see them being taken away from us. There are several impressions (that) occurred to me as soon as I heard about their death, and that is what I want to preach to my congregation this morning."

Tsiang went on to make several key points and cite scripture. One of his points:

> "We should speak to seek to please God, not men. As in Corinthians II 5:9 it says, 'Wherefore we labour, that whether present or absent,

對於雜克夫婦罹難的感想

一九七X年十二月X日蔣德恩牧師在新江紹興夫垮員伸堂講道

一月二十八日中航公司滬渝班第一四五號客機，在鄂西天門縣境失事墜毀該機共載乘客及機師二十六人，其中有两八十八小孩五人，婦女三人，僅一小孩受傷運滬治外，餘均慘遭四罹難深為惋惜，其中最可痛者為勞勤特維克夫婦二人，方由團神學院畢業來華，主服務，不幸亦遭殃及，氏夫婦為杭州西教士計高德先生夫婦與紹興西教士其耶士泰夫婦之友，都會在杭和他們一度會面，對於他倆離開祖國長途來華，為中國民眾服務的精神頗為欽佩，不料此次因中航機不慎失事，竟含苦永列心中大為難過，同時發生了許多感想，今天主日，在本堂全體教基友前，將我的感想分述於後。

一、人生在世，本是暫時的，真如詩篇第一四篇說：「人好像一口氣，他的年日，如同影兒快快過去。」所以我們應該常常注意，我們也要離開世界的在那一天離開，雖然不得而知，然而應當常常警醒預備！

二、每個人做人，要得主的喜悅，不是要得人的喜悅，所以哥林多後書第五章九節說：「所以無論是住在身內，離開身外，我們立定志向，要得主的喜悅。」如耶穌保羅和雜克夫等都是這樣。

三、世界上事有時不諧你的心，也不必難過，因為在不稱心的當中也許反能得到好的結果，所謂「塞翁失馬安知非福」。

像羅馬書第八章二十八節說：「萬事都互相効力，叫愛 上帝的人得益處。」所以我們無論是好是壞，我們如能愛 主都有益處。

四、以賽亞第四十章十三節說：「誰曾測度耶和華的心或作他的謀士指教他呢」所以這次雜克先生夫婦為 主服務，而遭遇此禍。上帝實已知道其中的一切計劃，我們人却不得而知，所以我們只能順從 上帝，因為出於 上帝的事沒有一椿不好的。

五、上帝也在教訓我們，應當萬事小心，這飛機的單禍患於不小心所致。天地之間物質有一定的定理，我們的靈心上也有一定的定理，我們都應該依照這定理而行，方能順利進行，否則就會遭禍，所以無論基督徒或非基督徒都應當照 上帝的定理而行。

六、雜克先生夫婦本身與其父母，或早已知道由華來服務，或將遇到危險，然而他們為愛耶穌的緣故，情願離開祖國來華傳教，所以他們的犧牲可說得是勇敢的犧牲，是為愛耶穌的緣故而犧牲，是我們最好的模範，真像使徒行傳第二十章二十四節所說：「使徒保羅就是為耶穌的緣故，死在耶路撒冷也是情願。」所以這次雜克先生夫婦來華工作，真是有使徒保羅傳道的精神。

以上六點，可作我們全體教善友的教訓，但願 上帝祝福他所遺下來的兒子，并在美的家屬！

The handwritten sermon given by T.E. Tsiang, pastor of the Shaohing Baptist Church in China.

93

A Sermon given by Pastor T. E. Tsiang
on Feb. 2, 1947 in Shaohing Baptist
Church in China.

"How the Death of the Vicks impressed me as a Christian?"
Scripture: Acts 21:7-14.

On Jan. 20, 1947 an aeroplane No. 145 dropped in the country
place of Hupeh Province where 26 died except one little child
was alive. Among the 26 people including pilots there were 11
foreigners, 5 children and 3 women. It was too bad to hear this
tragedy. Among the victims there were Mr. & Mrs. Vick and their
two children but later we found that the second child of theirs
was alive. I met for the first time the Vicks in Hangchow in
Jan. before they sailed for Chunchin. They were friends and
school mates of the Gilberts in Hangchow and the Nasmiths in Shaohing. The Vicks just graduated from Colgate Rochester Seminary
in the United States of America where I studied for one year too.
They came to China to help people to know Jesus Christ. I ad-
mired their spirit but I as well as all their friends felt very
very sorry to see them being taken away from us. There are several
impressions occurred to me as soon as I heard about their death
and that is what I want to preach to my congregation this morning.

1. No body can stay very long in this world. Just as in the Psalm
   144:4 it says, "Man is like to vanity: his days are as a shadow
   that passeth away." We do not know when we are going away &
   so we have to be on the watch all the time. God can take us
   away at any time.

2. We should seek to please God not men. As in II Corinthians
   5:9 it says, "Wherefore we labour, that whether present or ab-
   sent, we may be accepted of him." That was the aim of Jesus
   and Paul and others Christians when they were alive. The Vicks
   were so too, and we should be like them.

3. If things do not turn out as we wish do not feel bad about it
   because there might be some good out of it. How we wished
   their sail did not even succeed at first! How we wished they
   came to Shaohing to visit their friends and missed that plane?
   That they did not want to do because that was not their wish.
   However, we do our best and leave the results to God no matter
   whether they are good or bad because in Romans 8:28 it says,
   "And we know that all things work together for good to them
   that love God." Every thing comes from God to us is good.

4. We do not know God's wisdom and His plan for us and we have
   just to obey. As it says in Isaiah 40:13, "Who hath directed
   the Spirit of the Lord, or being his counsellor 4 hath taught
   him?" Obedience to God is the best policy.

5. There are laws in the Universe as well as in our spiritual life.
   We have to find those laws out with our might and main and do
   accordingly. So we have to be careful. There were some thing
   wrong in the plane which were not working according to the law
   and that killed people whether they were christians or not.

6. The Vicks and their family members might have guessed some dangers on their way to their destination. But the Vicks still
   came to China for Christ's sake. They were like Paul written
   in Acts 21:7-14. Praise to God! May God bless their family members!

*Marjorie Stannerd provided an English translation of T.E. Tsiang's sermon to
Jean Gilbert, who mailed it to Clarence and Ethel Vick. The title of the sermon
was "How the Death of the Vicks Impressed Me as a Christian."*

we may be accepted of him.' That was the aim of Jesus and Paul, and other Christians when they were alive. The Vicks were so, too, and we should be like them."

Later in the sermon he stated, "The Vicks and their family members might have guessed some dangers on their way to their destination. But the Vicks still came to China for Christ's sake."

In the congregation that day was Marjorie Stannerd, the wife of Ray Stannerd, a doctor in charge of the Baptist hospital in Shaohing. Marjorie Stannerd sent copies of Tsiang's sermon in both Chinese and English to Jean Gilbert along with a letter, all of which Jean mailed to my Vick grandparents. Stannerd shared her thoughts about hearing Tsiang's sermon:

"I could not help but feel, as I listened to him (and he is such a vigorous and forthright preacher) that Bob Vick and his wife were now speaking to the Chinese people, after only a few days in China, in such powerful language as they would not have dreamed of. They were not only speaking by their example in giving their lives, but they were speaking through Pastor Tsiang just the words they would gladly have spoken had they had them, and God seen fit to keep them here throughout a long life in China. It was not a sad or mournful service, but rather a powerful one...I could not help but think that in forty years of service in China, the Vicks could never have made their willingness to sacrifice their lives for the Gospel known to so many people. Every Chinese daily as well as all English ones have carried columns on the accident... We think longingly for the work that the Vicks would have done had they been permitted to live, but how can we know that the sum total of the value of their lives may not be greater in this short span? I know that every missionary feels that he is now under even greater obligation, doing not only what he can on his own account but an additional load in the name of the Vicks."

In Stannerd's letter to Jean Gilbert, she explained why she wanted the sermon sent to my father's parents:

"I thought if Bob Vick's parents knew of this contribution which their son and his family has made, probably not only in our community but doubtless all over China, that possibly they might wish to keep the notes of one such powerful sermon as a reminder

*that this tragedy which has stunned us all was not in vain but that
God used their gift of their lives for good even before they were in
their graves. I feel sure that both these young folks are rejoicing
even now that they were able to accomplish that for which they
dedicated their lives…I saw Bob for a moment the morning before
they took off (in Shanghai) and he was in high spirits. It's a nice
way to go, headed toward fulfillment of a dream and a purpose.
And who are we to say that it was not gloriously fulfilled?"*

Jean Gilbert also shared with my grandparents how she and Gordon
saw in my parents the "wonderful spirit of sacrificial devotion to whatever work lay ahead of them." The deaths of my parents created a void
as many missionaries were nearing the end of their last term and not
enough replacements were coming.

*"The challenge to us is to go beyond what we have felt able to
do before to help accomplish in a greater way their (Bob and
Dorothy's) hopes and aspirations for the Chinese people. It is our
prayer that the sacrifice which was required of them will challenge
also other young couples at home to give of themselves in preparation and volition to come take their place, and that what is now to
China a great loss in their going may become fulfillment of their
hopes and dreams by many others."*

My parents had touched many lives through my father's ministries
and their preparation to become missionaries. Grandpa and Grandma
Vick received more than 500 sympathy cards and letters, they told the
Gilberts in a letter in which they thanked them for the two letters they
had sent from Hangchow.

*"We can appreciate the shock the tragic news must have caused
you, particularly because they had so recently been with you. We do
thank you for the intimate account you gave us of their visit with
you, and how they were able to meet so many Mission folks while
there. We also appreciate the Shanghai newspaper clipping. This
together with your letters will be kept in the file of such things we
are preparing for Paul to read when he is old enough to do so. He
will have plenty of cause to be proud of his mother and dad…It was
especially thoughtful of you to copy for us part of Mrs. Stannerd's
wonderful letter and to send it with Pastor Tsiang's letter and his*

sermon notes in English and Chinese. How true it is that Bob and Dorothy were speaking to the Chinese people through Pastor Tsiang possibly more effectively than they could have in many years' work there... We pray that you may be very effective in your great calling."

A memorial service was held at Immanuel Baptist Church in the late afternoon on March 2, followed by another one that evening at East Penfield Baptist Church. Services were also held in Baldwinsville and at the Deep River Baptist Church in Connecticut, where my father preached while my parents studied at Yale.

The First Baptist Church of Summit, New Jersey, also held a service. This was the church where my parents had been commissioned as missionaries and which was substantially underwriting the Vick budget as missionaries. Rev. David K. Barnwell consoled those gathered:

"In the eyes of the world, it will seem that all their hopes and plans and preparations have been wasted and their lives brought to naught in a tragic finish. In our first shock of dismay, that may also be our feeling. It need not remain our feeling. To the eyes of Christian faith, there is infinitely more to be seen. There are old, old words of wisdom and insight that speak to us today, words of Saint Paul: 'We look not at the things which are seen, but at the unseen; for the things which are seen are temporal, but the things which are not seen are eternal.'

"For one thing the work of Robert and Dorothy Vick among us here is not finished. Their brief visits to us gave us something that lives among us. They were so very genuine. With the utmost simplicity and clarity they told us of their desire to serve Christ and His kingdom. We could not help but see in them the singleness of heart, the purity of spirit, the sincerity of dedication that marked their lives. Quietly, without any shadow of ostentation, it was self-evident to all of us who talked with them, and listened to them, that they had consecrated their lives completely to the Lord of Life...

"As one of you said to me this week, it is good to have known them. Our church is blessed to have had them for a little while... We know that the lives of Robert and Dorothy and little Teddy have not ended. In the great eternal economy of God, their preparation, their service, is not wasted."

Grandpa Vick shared that sentiment. In *The Worth of a Life* booklet, he is quoted as saying, a few days after hearing the news of the plane crash:

"Of course we should have memorial services, but ours must be more than remembering. We must turn it all to good. We must do something in the name of Robert and Dorothy to advance the cause of Christ in China."

Not surprisingly, many people of deep faith concurred, including Rev. Barnwell, Rev. Osgoode H. McDonald, then pastor of Immanuel, and the American Baptist Foreign Mission Society board. After discussion that included my grandparents, the ABFMS announced the creation of "The Robert and Dorothy Vick Memorial Fund" to be used for training American and Chinese students for missionary work in China for twenty-five years, the length of time that my parents were expected to serve there.

I think my parents would have been very pleased with this memorial. When news of the crash arrived at the ABFMS office in New York City, a letter that my father had written on Dec. 28, 1946 on board the *Marine Lynx* was being mimeographed for distribution to be sent to friends. In the letter, my father detailed some of my parents' experiences on the car trip to San Francisco and then their time aboard the *Marine Lynx*, which was about to enter the inland waters of the China Sea from the Pacific Ocean on the day that my father was writing to friends back home.

He concludes his letter with this:

"Through all of this experience we have felt the strength which comes from your prayers. As I have been writing this letter, I have had your names before me, thinking of each of you and the work we are doing. As I write these letters from time to time, I shall do so with the view of including those things in which you—each of you—will be especially interested. In return, we want your letters, your questions, and your suggestions. We are, in a real sense, your representatives in China. We don't know as yet what experiences await us. We expect to find a most turbulent country. We know we shall be finding a country where the loving Christ has gone on ahead and is patiently beckoning us to come on and minister in His name and His strength. And so, fortified by your prayers, and acknowledging Him as our only strength, we move on.

"Yours in service, Robert A. Vick."

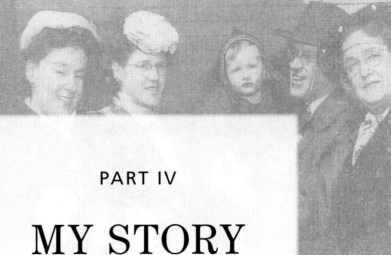

e Paul Vick on Last Lap of China-to-Rochester Trip

ed little boy who has
more adventure into his
s and six months of life
st people do in a lifetime
the last lap of a long trip
Rochester today.

Ashton Vick, sole survivor
plane crash in China which
persons, including his par-
e Rev. and Mrs. Robert A.
and his three-year-old
Teddy, arrived yesterday
in New York City by air
s Angeles. He was met i
ndparents, Mr. and M
A. Vick of 142 Harve

on hand to greet the b
s two aunts, Mrs. Earl
of Webster, and Mrs. G
Henry of Kendall, as w
esentatives of the Childre
ciety, Paul's grandparer
was entirely recovered fr
ctures, suffered in the
ast Jan. 28. His life w
when his father, a missi
aped from the plane w
oy in his arms. The fat
r 40 hours and directed t
be sent to his grandpare
hester.
e Vick home today it w
at the party is expec
me tonight. They plann
in Baldwinsville to v
maternal grandparents,
rs. Lester Flanders. At

Mrs. Gordon E. Henry, M
r. and Mrs. Clarence A. V

ildren of the Happs, to keep
mpany. The child was f
ross the Pacific from Shan

PART IV
MY STORY

amily

February 10, 1971   Section

Want Ads on Page 6

e Streets

THE PRIEST CALLS

day late this summer Paul and his
arents had a caller. It was Rev
el McCarthy, Roman Catholic mis
y of China. Passing through th
States on his way to his native tow
bbereen, County Cork, Ireland, o
t leave in 17 years, Father McCarth
a special point of going to see th

was Father McCarthy who led th
of Paul and his father from th
of the tragic plane crash. He saw t
e of Bob Vick during the hours o
hat remained to him and of Pau
could be taken to a Shanghai hos

receives top Philanthropy Award

apraised fot was starting an
other   a silhouette of Black
Panther Leader Bobby Seale.
In the next room, a shaggy-
haired white youth in a black
felt hat with a beaded band
was painting a mural of a
guru-type man, complete with
long hair and love beads.
"If you think this is bad, you
ought to see the embalming
room." Tim Spinning said,
looking up from his paint. He
stopped long enough to explain
why he's helping convert the
old ex-funeral home at
South Ave. into a youth-crime
control center.
"We want a 24-hour switch-
board here, where kids can
freaked out on
drugs   want a place
where   ys can stay
overnight   y're had an ar-
ment or some-

PAUL VICK
This is street work . . .

He and about a dozen other
teenagers, adult volunteers
and youth workers have sp
the last four weeks fixing
two-story Frick

SEAC]. It will be SEAC's
main center in a program to
combat juvenile delinquency
and drug abuse in southern
Rochester.

A similar center, operated
by the 19th Ward Community
Association, will serve teenagers on the southwe
of the river in a
cated across from
School.
Both are part of
program covering
ern half of the city
York State Crime Co
provided $126,000
money, with SEAC,
Ward Association a
Memorial Hospital
the rest.
"This is one of t
eeds in Roches

Middle Earth: A Sound

Young people who phone or drop
in to Middle Earth at any time
of the day are able to talk with
the paraprofessional counselors
about anything.
"We get problems of loneli-
ness, sex, drugs, parents, legal
matters, just about anything,"
says Steve Wirth, one of the two
coordinators on the staff. "I've
heard so many problems that I'm
not surprised by anything any-
more."
The counseling, Wirth empha-
sizes, is not advice-giving.
"If someone comes in and wanted to get to the bus stop, I'd
probably tell him that," Wirth
smiled, "but we make it clear
to anyone who comes in with
a problem that we won't solve
it for him. We can mirror to
people what they are; they can
do with the

Sixteen Years Later

Sixteen years ago, on Jan. 28,
1947, an airplane crash in
China took the lives of the
Rev. and Mrs. Robert A. Vick,
American Baptist missionaries,
and one son. Another son, Paul,
then 18 months old, survived.
Today that youngster is a
high school senior in Rochester,
N.Y., where he lives with his
grandparents, Mr. and Mrs.
Clarence Vick.
President of the Baptist
Youth Fellowship at Immanuel
Baptist Church, in Rochester,
he has raised more than $500
to send seven students to Green
Lake this summer.
"Paul is a fine young man,
red-headed and tall and shows
leadership ability," writes

arth is forging
e connection,
rth in a youth pro
by five full-tim
four VISTA volu
Arm forever funeral
South Ave.
bout four years ago

He plans to enter college in
the fall and plans to enter
philosophy, sociology or

as a recreation-oriented agency
known as the Southeast Ecumenical Youth Ministry, the Middle
Earth Youth Project has dropped
all affiliation with organized religion and has switched its em-
phasis from recreation to counseling.

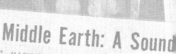

Chapter 13

The Beginning of My Journey

As I look back over the past seventy-five years, I have grown increasingly aware of the extent the events of seventy-four years ago have shaped my life. As often the case, this insight was not immediately apparent to me, although it should have been. I have no recollection (at least that I am aware of), of the plane crash that took the lives of so many, including my father, mother, and brother. Nor do I have recollection of my return to the United States and subsequent arrival at the home of my father's parents, where I would spend the next twenty years of my life. Any knowledge I have comes from family, friends, and those who knew my parents and brother as well as from newspaper and magazine articles, my parent's personal papers, and hundreds of letters.

Curiously, it was not until a few years ago that I pulled out boxes containing these letters, articles, and other documents recording events in the life of my parents, their call to the mission field, their preparation to serve, their arrival in China, and their death en route to their first mission assignment. Many of these records came from my father's and mother's parents, while others had been received from time to time through the years from those who had known my parents or were personally involved in some of those events. I am not sure why I kept those boxes sealed for so many years. Perhaps in some way I knew that once I opened those boxes, I would be peeling back layers that would unleash emotions deeply buried within me and set me on a path where there was no turning back.

After my return from China, my father's sisters agreed they would assist my Vick grandparents in raising me. Suddenly, my grandparents, now in their 60s, found themselves taking on the responsibility of raising an 18-month-old toddler. Fortunately, their two daughters lived close by. My Aunt Bubbles and Uncle Earl Happ had built a home in Webster, about ten miles north of Rochester. They had two children at the time and were expecting a third (subsequently two more children were born), and had no difficulty accommodating another from time to time.

My Aunt Carol and Uncle Gordon Henry were living with his parents in Kendall, about 35 miles northwest of Rochester. They had one son, Randy, who was nineteen days older than me. My uncle was considering opening an auto repair shop and had begun looking at possible locations. Grandpa Vick had expressed a willingness to assist him, so the family decided that the Henrys would move into the home on Harvard Street until a location for the shop was found. Aunt Carol would be able to take care of both her son and me while my grandparents were at work.

Eventually, my uncle found an ideal location for the business—a triangular section of land in the village of Victor, approximately seventeen miles southeast of Rochester. In addition to a gas station and garage, there was a small house immediately to the right of the garage and a large two-story duplex on the corner, which would provide rental income. Once the property was purchased, I moved with them to Victor. They stayed in this property for a little over ten years until after the birth of two more children. They then moved to a larger farm house outside the village of Victor.

A young Paul Vick in front of his Vick grandparents' 1949 Oldsmobile Rocket 88 in the driveway of their home at 142 Harvard St.

For two years, I lived with Aunt Carol and Uncle Gordon during the week. While I have little memory of those first couple of years, I am told that my Aunt Carol often hooked my cousin and me to a harness when running errands or simply going out for a walk. On weekends, both my cousin and I traveled back to Rochester and stayed with our grandparents. At some point, my cousin and I began going to the YMCA, only a few blocks from my house on Monroe Avenue, each Saturday. We would spend the morning in the gym and then head to the pool in the basement. There was a black-and-white TV set up in the lounge area where we were introduced to Flash Gordon, Hopalong Cassidy, Roy Rogers, and other such early TV classics. On Sundays, the Happs and Henrys would join us for church at Immanuel Baptist and then we would head out to Webster for Sunday dinner before my cousin and I would return to Victor.

Although I have no memory of it, Father Michael McCarthy, the Catholic missionary who had ministered to my father as he was dying, visited Grandpa and Grandma Vick and me in July 1948. A story in the *Democrat and Chronicle* newspaper stated that he stopped in Rochester on his way to his hometown in Ireland, having flown to the United States from China. "Rochester should be proud of the Rev. Mr. Vick," Father McCarthy is quoted as saying. "He was a fine Christian man."

Father Michael McCarthy, right, was so moved by his experience of ministering to Robert Vick after the plane crash that he visited the Vicks on his way from China to Ireland in July 1948. It was the first time he'd seen Paul since Paul's transfer to Shanghai for medical care after the plane crash. Photo of Paul and Clarence Vick and Father McCarthy taken outside the home of Paul's uncle and aunt, Earl and Ruth Happ, in Webster.

*   *   *

Beginning in the fall of 1949 when I was about four years old, I began living with my grandparents full time. I attended nursery school at a nearby private girl's school that accepted boys through Kindergarten. When the parents of Grandma Vick had died, they had left the house at 142 Harvard St. equally to Grandma Vick and her brother, my great-uncle, George, who was eight years older than his sister, having been born in 1873. Uncle George had spent his entire life living in that home, and so he had been an integral part in the life of my father, my aunts, and now me. He was included in all family events, and we all felt a strong bond of affection for him. He occupied a central part in the lives of all of us cousins. On one occasion, upon returning from a week attending the Pastor's and Layman's Conference at Keuka College with our grandparents, several of us cousins raced into the house. I was the first to run into the kitchen where Uncle George was having breakfast, sitting on a stool in his usual place at the end of a kitchen cupboard/sideboard. I was so excited to see him that I threw myself at him to give him a hug. Taken by surprise, he was not prepared to receive such an onslaught and was knocked off his stool; he ended up sitting in his spilt coffee and cereal.

However, there was a big bone of contention, particularly with Grandma Vick, with Uncle George's constant smoking of cigars. She often came home from work and threw a fit because of the thick fog of smoke that enveloped the living room where he sat much of the day. One of his favorite cigars was Muriel Senators. Many a time Uncle George asked me to go to a local drug store and pick up a box for him. On two or three occasions I snuck a cigar out of the house and lit it up in the garage. This experiment did not last long, as I turned green after only a few puffs.

A favorite location in our home, not only for Uncle George but also for Grandma Vick, was the side porch. A trestle covered with morning glories created an "outside wall" to the porch. Bees and wasps seemed to enjoy the morning glories as much as we did. Bees and wasps enjoyed sunning themselves on my uncle's shoulder. He paid them no mind. He always maintained that if you didn't bother them, they wouldn't bother you.

The first time I memorized scripture was on that porch. One day one of my cousins and I were sitting on the porch talking with Grandma Vick. Somehow, the topic of scripture came up. Grandma Vick challenged us to memorize Psalm 23. If we were able to accomplish that task, she would give a quarter to each of us. By the end of the day, we each were twenty-five cents richer.

I don't remember Uncle George ever saying a cross word or uttering a complaint. He was extremely tolerant, patient, and low-key. This was borne out in his efforts to teach me his trade of painting and wallpapering. He kept his equipment in a shed behind the house. There were shelves of leftover wallpaper, and the shed smelled of turpentine and old paint. Even though Uncle George was in his late 70s when I came to live with my grandparents, he still did the painting and wallpapering needed to maintain the house. I have an early memory of him painting the outside of the house. When I asked if I could help, he handed me a brush and then showed me how much paint to put on the brush and the correct way to apply the paint. (I can't recall how well I did, but I suspect he painted over my efforts when I was not looking.) The most important lesson he taught me was the cleaning of the equipment, especially brushes, to preserve them for future use. As he got older and he could no longer do the painting and wallpapering in the house, I took over that responsibility but always under his watchful eye.

Two months after his 90th birthday, in September 1963, Uncle George passed away. For the last several months of his life, he resided in Kirkhaven Nursing Home on Park Avenue, within walking distance of our home. I had just left for college in Kalamazoo, Michigan, when I received word of his death. I was told that just before he died, he asked where I was. Tears still come to my eyes when I think of that time when I was not there for him.

The big old house at 142 Harvard St. was a touchstone for me as well as a gathering place for the entire family. The two-story house that my family acquired in the mid-nineteenth century was long and narrow. A smaller version of the house had been moved from the corner of Goodman and Brighton streets one block south to Harvard Street around the turn of the century to make room for an apartment building; it became the second house located on that section of Harvard Street. A two-story addition created space for a new kitchen on the first floor, and a bedroom and bathroom on the second floor.

One of those special times of family gatherings occurred every Christmas Day. The tradition was that each family opened presents in their own homes on Christmas morning. For me, this meant waking up early and coming down the stairs in eager anticipation. I

The Vick family had a long-standing tradition of celebrating Christmas together. Paul with Clarence and Ethel Vick at the home of Earl and Ruth Happ around 1950.

marveled at all the presents, which mysteriously had appeared under the tree the previous night. I first, however, took my stocking down from where it had been hung on the chimney, which ran up the wall of our dining room. Looking at that stocking today it seems fairly small. But then it held socks, small toys, and generally an orange and other fruit.

My aunts, uncles, and cousins arrived in the early afternoon. Each brought some part of the meal. We always had turkey, which Grandpa Vick had prepared early that day while Grandma Vick made the dressing. It was pure chaos when my cousins arrived. Because presents were not to be opened until after dinner (which generally was not served until mid-afternoon), we kids had the run of the upstairs or played outside. Waiting to open presents was pure agony. We were sure that the parents and grandparents were in conspiracy to draw out the meal and its preparation as long as possible.

It was amazing how fast we kids could consume food once it was placed on the table. The adults, however, were not as quick to finish the meal, and then they insisted on cleaning up and washing dishes before we could open the presents. The pile of presents under the tree grew considerably with the addition of those from Victor and Webster. As all kids do, we gathered around the tree trying to guess what might be in the wrapped packages.

After what seemed an eternity, everyone finally congregated in the living room and front room. A free-for-all then began. Before you knew it, paper and boxes were strewn all over the place. After the family cleaned up the rooms and stacked and placed the presents in bags, it was time for dessert. There were generally two options, Christmas pudding or ice cream.

Christmas pudding was a long-held tradition in the Vick family. A couple of days before Christmas, Grandma Vick bought lard that she mixed with flour, ginger, raisins, and other ingredients, and then placed the mixture in a cloth sack and boiled it in water on the stovetop. She made a hot white lemon sauce, which was spooned on top of the pudding in each dish to be served. Most of us kids would take an obligatory bite of the pudding and then quickly switch to the ice cream.

This tradition of celebrating Christmas on Harvard Street continued even after many of us left our respective homes. The last year we gathered on Harvard Street was 1968. Grandpa Vick died the following May, and Grandma Vick went to live with Aunt Carol in Victor. Beginning in 1969 and continuing until 2002, a Christmas day family gathering in the evening continued at the Webster home of Aunt Bubbles and Uncle Earl's home, until it became too much for Aunt Bubbles. Beginning in 2003 and continuing to this day, the families still gather in the evening on Christmas day for dessert at the home of my wife and me. A tradition that began as long ago as I can remember has now been experienced by four generations.

*   *   *

In the living room of our home on Harvard Street was an upright piano that Grandma Vick sometimes played. When I entered first grade, I began to take piano lessons. Although I enjoyed listening to music, I didn't have the discipline to practice. Realizing that my future as a pianist was quite limited, Grandma Vick brought out my father's violin when I was in third grade, and I began to take lessons at school. Fortunately for Uncle George, I practiced in the upstairs front room that had become my room, not in the living room. Although I never became very accomplished, I thoroughly enjoyed playing the violin. I played in the school orchestra through elementary school and high school. As with the piano, practice was my weak point. At some point in high school, the orchestra conductor, Mr. Howe, gave me an ultimatum—either take individual lessons with him or drop out. I took the lessons.

The cellar of this old house was a scary place for a small child. Part of the cellar had a concrete floor, but toward the front of the house, the floor was still dirt until a concrete floor was installed at some point during my early years. Under the stairs was the potato bin. To the left of the stairs was a fruit cellar containing jars of canned fruit and vegetables. On the other side of the fruit cellar were stairs to the outside through two doors that swung up. Every week I pulled cans of ashes from our coal-fired furnace and hauled them up the stairs. A truck made regular deliveries of coal by placing a chute through the basement window and dumping the allotted load down the chute into the coal bin. Uncle George and Grandpa Vick then shoveled coal into the furnace. At some point, an automatic coal feeder was installed, obviating the need to shovel coal into the furnace. Since there was no system to automatically empty the ashes, I continued to perform that chore until the coal-burning furnace was replaced with a gas-burning one in the late 1950s.

It wasn't until I was 12 or 13 years old that I found another use for the basement. I set up a "chemistry lab" toward the front of the basement, complete with Bunsen burners, flasks, and beakers. A good friend of mine, whom I had known throughout elementary school, and I set about experimenting with different chemicals purchased from a company that we could reach by bike. One of our experiments was making gun powder. One day, after mixing the appropriate chemicals, we decided to run a test. We packed the gunpowder into a pipe and constructed a fuse. We placed the pipe in the backyard near the garage, lit the fuse, and made a beeline for the house. Unfortunately, the experiment was a success. The explosion was heard all through the neighborhood and shattered the garage window. Not long after, we spotted a police car slowly proceeding down our street. Somehow, my friend and I escaped scrutiny, and no one learned the cause of the explosion. I can't remember what excuse I gave my grandparents about the broken window. I do know this was the last experiment I undertook.

We ate most of our meals at the kitchen table in the center of the kitchen. Upon returning from school in the afternoon, I often fixed myself a sandwich. I was thrilled when we had tongue for dinner as I was able to fry up leftovers. With a little mustard, I treated myself to a tremendous after-school snack. Spam or hot dogs fried up were an acceptable alternative. My grandparents generally arrived home from the office around 5:30 p.m., with dinner ready by 6. Dinner was a time of family discussion and catching up on the day's events. Then it was time for washing, drying, and putting away the dishes before we each went off to work on whatever we had to do. Often my grandparents went out to make business calls or attend some event at church or some other Baptist gathering. When I was younger, I sometimes went with them. Most of the time I remained around the house or played with friends until it was bed time.

*   *   *

At some point during my early years in elementary school, my grandparents let me pick out a dog as a pet. I chose the runt of the litter. She was black with a white patch on her chest. I named her Topsy. We built a kennel in the backyard complete with doghouse. Although we did everything we could to keep her in the kennel, she managed to find a way out.

Gathering around Paul and the Happs' beloved St. Bernard named Pam are from left, George Thompson (Paul's great-uncle), and grandparents Esther and Lester Flanders and Ethel and Clarence Vick.

Often on my way home from school, I would see her running down the street to greet me. She was my constant companion. We did everything together. One day when I arrived home from school, I found her laying on the ground in obvious pain. It turned out that she had eaten poison, and before long she died. I was devastated. My grandparents soon took me to take a look at a newborn litter of puppies. I fell in love with the runt of that litter, too. She even looked like Topsy. I named her Cindy (after a cousin of one of my friends for whom I had developed quite a crush). She had the same loveable disposition as Topsy but also had the same ability to escape the kennel. About a year later, while I was visiting my cousins in Victor, my grandparents called to tell me that Cindy had been hit by a car and had died. The death of Cindy had an even more profound impact on me than the loss of Topsy. I did not have another pet until my days in seminary.

Two rooms on the second floor at the front of the house became mine. There was a small room overlooking the front porch that could not have been more than five feet by eight feet that served as my bedroom. That small room opened to a larger room situated over the front room. When my father and aunts were growing up, the small room had been Aunt Carol's room while the larger room belonged to Aunt Bubbles. My father's bedroom was adjacent to this larger room heading toward the back of the house. Although a door connected my father's room to his older sister's room, fortunately, there was another door leading to the second-floor balcony. Unfortunately, Aunt Carol had no other way to her small cubicle other than through her sister's room. As I was the only child during my growing up years, I had no such challenges to navigate through.

As no significant heat reached the little nook that served as my bedroom, during the winter months I burrowed under a pile of blankets providing not only warmth but also a sense of security. The house was huge, especially for a young child, and old, full of creaks and groans.

During my younger years, at bedtime, Grandpa Vick often sat on my bed and read to me from books containing nursery rhymes, animal stories, classical tales, myths and legends, nature stories, character sketches, heroes and patriots, poems, prayers, and Bible stories. The magic and imagery of these stories took me to other worlds where fantasy and reality blended, giving free rein to my imagination. Thankfully, I had the blankets to burrow under when the light went off and Grandpa

Vick went downstairs! For a small child, noises of a creaking old house conjured up all sorts of monsters just waiting to pounce on me.

During my early years, Grandpa Vick slept in the bedroom my father had occupied. Although the master bedroom was at the back of the house, I am pretty sure Grandpa Vick took to sleeping in my father's room to be closer to me in case I had a problem during the night. When I got older, he moved back to his own bedroom, staying in this bedroom only during times either he or Grandma Vick were ill.

I sometimes took naps in my grandparents' bedroom. During one of the times, when I supposedly was napping, I began to fool around with the large cabinet radio next to the bed. I accidently broke one of the dials. When my grandparents later questioned me about the broken dial, I at first denied any knowledge. Eventually I fessed up and admitted that I had done it. As punishment, my grandparents made me stay on the bed and think about what lying meant and the importance of being able to be trusted. This was a lesson I never forgot.

*   *   *

My nursery school was located in a red wooden building behind the Columbia Girls School on South Goodman Street next to the Rochester Museum and Science Center. I attended kindergarten in the main building. The two most vivid memories I have are the naps taken on the gym floor and a wide, stone veranda in the front of the building where I waited for my grandparents to pick me up on their way home from work. During this time I was invited to my first birthday party at the home of a classmate who lived on Lake Ontario next to Durand Eastman beach. Another first experience connected with Columbia occurred many years later when I was invited by the very same cousin of one of my friends (after whom I had named my second dog) to a dance at the school. Many of the staff remembered me, which created the feeling of a homecoming of sorts. Years later, the headmistress of the school became a client of mine.

I entered first grade in 1951 at School #23 where I spent the next seven years. The school was located a little over a half mile from our home. The first two or three days of that first year, Grandpa Vick walked with me to school to make sure I knew the way and how to find my way home. After that I was on my own, but I do not recall ever getting lost.

During my first few years at School #23, I was more interested in having fun then studying. In the classroom I kept my head down and avoided getting into trouble. I did just enough to get by until fifth grade. The first marking period resulted in no passing grades. The school recommended that my grandparents find a tutor for me. A retired teacher who lived a couple of miles from school agreed to undertake this formidable task. For several months, twice a week, I trekked to her house. The tutoring must have worked, because my grades improved considerably by the end of the year. By seventh grade, my grades had improved sufficiently for me to be selected as a crossing guard. One of my proudest moments was being given the white belt to be worn across my chest.

Every Saturday afternoon, Uncle George and my grandparents continued the tradition of heading out to Victor so I could spend time with my cousins. Sunday mornings we attended Immanuel Baptist Church. After church, we drove to Webster for Sunday dinner, followed by an afternoon of play with the Webster cousins. During the warmer months, a pond situated on a neighbor's property served as a source for catching bullfrogs. Much to the consternation of Aunt Bubbles, she periodically came upon a bucket of croaking frogs. An even greater commotion arose if she discovered a frog mistakenly left in a pants pocket. During the winter, we shoveled off the snow on the pond and created an

FRANCIS PARKER SCHOOL #23 1958

Paul, in the back row fifth from left, attended Frances Parker School #23, located a little more than a half mile from the home of his Vick grandparents. One of his proudest moments was being selected to be a crossing guard.

ice rink where hotly contested ice hockey was played. Often, we made our way to Webster Park and took advantage of a great hill for sledding and tobogganing. Sunday evenings we attended Baptist Youth Fellowship at Webster Baptist Church. When I reached high school, we returned earlier to Rochester so I could attend the youth group at Immanuel.

I spent considerably more time in Webster during school breaks because there were more than 500 acres of forest connected to the property, which served as a children's paradise. Uncle Earl had built a tennis court with a gravel surface with high chicken wire backstops on either end where we spent hours learning to play tennis. In a field just beyond the tennis court, a baseball diamond was laid out where we enjoyed playing baseball. As the roads in the area were not well-traveled, we frequently rode bikes throughout the countryside. When we heard the whistle of a locomotive sounding off, we rushed down to the railroad tracks to watch it go by. By the time we had graduated from high school, both the locomotives and the tracks were gone. But as a small child, watching those huge locomotives rumble by was magical.

Playing outdoors in the forest adjacent to the Happ property provided countless hours of fun. Skating one winter's day are Paul, second from right, with his Happ cousins, from left: Robert, Ronald, David, and Sharon.

Paul's maternal grandfather, Lester Flanders, co-owned the Mercer Milling Company, located adjacent to the Seneca River in Baldwinsville, New York. Paul spent school and summer vacations with his grandfather, learning not just about the mill from him, but life lessons on dealing with adversity.

*   *   *

My time with my mother's family was limited to school breaks and summer recess. As I mentioned previously, Grandpa Flanders was an owner of Mercer Milling Company located on the Seneca River and adjacent to a water falls in Baldwinsville. The mill was operated by large turbines, originally powered by water flow, but later supplemented by electricity. During my early years, much of my time visiting Grandpa Flanders was spent in the mill and going with him on trips to bakeries and stores throughout central New York where he took orders for flour delivery. Visiting these bakeries was like visiting a gold mine. The bakery staff couldn't resist this little red-headed freckled kid. I ended up with more baked goods than I could ever consume.

Those trips, often lasting two to three days, were special because of the bond that was created between Grandpa Flanders and me. Grandpa Flanders had a warm, outgoing personality textured with wit and humor. He seemed to find joy in the moments we shared and he told stories conveying life lessons. Although our time together was limited, there is probably no one who influenced my life more than he did. By seeing the way he lived his life and learning of the tragedies he endured, I came to understand that it is not adversity that defines our lives but what we do with adversity.

The sights, sounds, and smells of the mill have stayed with me throughout my life. When not traveling with Grandpa Flanders, I spent significant time exploring the nooks and crannies of the four-story structure. The milling process fascinated me. The transformation from grain to flour unfolded before my eyes. Trucks dumped grain into shafts built into the front docks. Elevators then transported grain to the top floor, where it was ground by a large millstone. The grain was then loaded onto elevators that transported it to lower levels where it would be checked and then sent back up for further grinding and the adding of different ingredients. This process continued until the miller was satisfied that the right texture had been reached.

The grain then was packed into five-, twenty-five-, and fifty-pound bags and transported by hand carts to a storage area and later loaded onto trucks for distribution. As I grew older, I was allowed to fill and paste the small bags, and I learned to tie the larger burlap bags with the miller's knot. At times when the trucks needed to be loaded, I joined in loading the hand trucks and transporting them onto the truck. As I think back, I am amazed that a child of my age was given free rein to roam unsupervised through the mill among moving conveyor belts, grain elevators, and other milling machinery. For me, it was like being transported to an earlier time in a place that had existed well over 100 years.

The Flanders had a tradition of holding a reunion every five years near the old family homestead in Sherwood, Michigan. This started as a way for Grandpa Flanders and his six siblings and their offspring to remain connected with their parents, Calvin and Ida Flanders, and each other. My first trip to the reunion, which I remember, was held in 1950, although I believe I was taken to a reunion by my parents before leaving for China. Two of Grandpa Flanders' siblings, Uncle Zoe and Aunt Leatha, still lived on small dairy farms. When I was young, I asked Uncle

Zoe if I could go out with him to milk the cows. He obliged by waking me up by lantern at 4:00 a.m. For some reason, I found the idea less exciting than the night before. Although he only had several milk cows, he still milked by hand. As I watched him milk each cow, it seemed quite easy. When he approached the last cow, he suggested I give a hand at it. Try as I might, I never was able to master the required technique. I could have sworn the cow gave me a disgusted look. The next chore was cleaning the cow manure from the troughs and loading it onto a manure spreader to be distributed across the fields. That was a task I could accomplish. The reward was a huge breakfast—platters of fried eggs, bacon, potatoes, and toast.

Over the years, the reunions grew as families grew, easily exceeding 100 relatives. Grandpa Flanders organized trips to the farms where he and his siblings were raised. He shared many stories of life on the farm, some of which are set forth in another section of these memoirs. The last reunion Grandpa Flanders attended was in 1981. He was the last living child of Calvin and Ida, and it was likely he would not live to the next one. The entire family liked and respected him, which made this reunion extra special. Lee Flanders, my uncle, took over the responsibility of organizing the reunions, and so they continued after Grandpa Flanders' death until a few years ago.

Although he was my uncle, Lee was closer in age to me (being ten years older) than he was to my mother (being fourteen years younger), so he was more like an older brother. An early memory is me tagging along on a hike with Lee's Scout troop in Baldwinsville. Hiking, as it turns out, became a lifelong passion of Lee's. More often than not, through the intervening years, when we were together, there was a trail somewhere that we would explore. Lee's love of nature and the outdoors opened another opportunity for me. After Lee graduated from Cornell University, the Audubon Society hired him to coordinate educational opportunities at the Ipswich River Wildlife Sanctuary and Pleasant Valley Wildlife Sanctuary, both in Massachusetts. I spent time with him at both locations and was introduced to birds and other wildlife through summer programs he ran at each site. He also introduced me to live philharmonic concerts. While at Pleasant Valley, Lee ushered for the Boston Pops concerts at Tanglewood, providing me with free entry to hear live classical concerts conducted by Arthur Fiedler.

*   *   *

Every summer for a week, my Vick grandparents, several cousins, and I attended the Pastor's and Layman's Conference at Keuka College. We stayed in one of the old dorm rooms in Ball Hall (one of the three main buildings comprising the college at the time), sleeping on metal cots with a communal bathroom on the floor. Meals were served on the lower level of that building overlooking a long walkway to Keuka Lake. At meal times, the hallway leading to stairs to the lower level filled up with people waiting for the doors to open. The director of the conference led us in song, devotions, and prayer at every meal. Occasionally, someone brought out a saw and played music with a bow, always a crowd favorite.

In the mornings, a bus took the kids to the First Baptist Church in Penn Yan for vacation bible school. One of the crafts I vividly recall was making paper mâché puppet heads and then attaching a cloth to the head. We then participated in a puppet show for the conference attendees. After returning from Penn Yan, eating lunch and resting, we headed to the lake for a couple of hours of swimming. During free time we explored areas in and around the college campus. Hagedorn Hall, the academic building, was a popular spot to explore. As nursing was a major program at Keuka, of particular interest to us were the labs where plastic skeletal structures and other anatomical replicas were kept behind glass doors in cabinets. The gym was in the basement of this building. Fencing must have been a popular sport as the walls of one room were lined with fencing masks and swords, conjuring up impressive images for a young child.

Each year a talent show was held in a red barn that served as the playhouse for the college. One year, two of my cousins and I decided to perform as a trio. I played the violin, while one cousin played the trombone and another the clarinet. While my two cousins were fairly accomplished (one eventually played the trombone in the Navy band and conducted one of the Navy bands), my musicality left much to be desired. This remains one of the more embarrassing moments of my life.

I also attended sessions at Camp Vick, one of our state church camps named after my family. The camp was established in the early 1950s on approximately 240 acres located ninety minutes south of Rochester. The only structure on the land when acquired was a stone hunting lodge over-looking a man-made lake that was annually stocked with fish. A portable structure added to the hunting lodge created a dining area. Eventually a

Paul with Grandma Vick and his cousin Randy Henry at Camp Vick, a Baptist camp established in 1953 in the memory of Paul's parents and brother and located on 240 acres in Sandusky, New York, southwest of Rochester. Paul recalls fond memories of attending the camp as a youngster and participating in its many activities that ranged from Bible studies to boating on the man-made lake. The camp still operates today.

The Baptist New Yorker   September, 1950

Hit The Trail For Greater Baptist Camping

For 20 years Baptist camping in New York State has been advancing. Along wooded trails our boys and girls have come in growing numbers to know Christ as Lord of their lives. The finest Christian leaders of our churches frequently claim to have met the Saviour beside a lake, in a campfire circle, under the stars at one of our camping programs.

The time has come to take the next step forward and establish our own campsites where the rich traditions of our denomination and its great heritage may become implanted; where the numbers of young people challenged and trained may increase.

Two properties have been purchased. One, already equipped, is located on Otsego Lake, Cooperstown. The other, a 190-acre farm, is located near Hermitage. The program contemplates the building up of both sites into beautiful and modern camps.

WESTERN SITE TO BE MEMORIAL TO THE VICKS

The Western site will be dedicated as a memorial to Robert and Dorothy Vick. Bob Vick made his commitment to the missionary cause years ago at one of our camping programs. The heroic lives of these two young martyrs will continue to inspire new generations of Christian youth.

Located in the beautiful rolling terrain of Wyoming County, the future Baptist campsite for western New York comprises 190 acres. It is near the village of Hermitage, and is 57 miles from Rochester, 46 miles from Buffalo, 85 miles from Jamestown, and 55 miles from Olean.

An artificial lake will provide for the swimming at camp. A main lodge with a well-equipped kitchen, dining space for about 150 persons, and a large assembly hall will occupy the center of the site. Four "villages," each with two tents or tepees will provide living space for four counselors and twenty-eight campers. A 28-acre maple grove provides the setting for three of these "units."

Health lodge and staff cabins will be built near the main lodge. An outdoor chapel will provide a place for vesper services—with the sunset over distant hills as the worship center.

Some churches will want to undertake specific projects, such as the building of a cabin, or the landscaping of the chapel. Some farmer's groups, in work-camp style, will build some of the cabins. This is a cooperative venture and all contributions of work or money will find a useful part to play.

Conklin to Head Campaign

The Rev. T. L. Conklin, known widely as "Pastor Ted," younger of Pathfinder Lodge, will be executive director for the fund-raising drive. Mr. Conklin is pastor of the First Baptist Church of Cooperstown. The people of his parish have generously granted him a one-year leave of absence, to do this important task. No one is more closely identified in the hearts of our people with Baptist camping than is "Pastor Ted," who founded Camp Nepwraca for boys 21 years ago.

He will be assisted by a Camp Campaign Committee made up of the Rev. Victor Kane, of Niagara Falls, chairman; Mr. Ray Robinson, Watertown; Mr. Don Merwin, Utica, and Mr. Albert Scheeline, Sanborn.

CAMPAIGN GOAL — $125,000

A goal of $125,000 has been set for this great undertaking. Approximately $85,000 will be available to build Camp Vick and $40,000, to complete Pathfinder Lodge.

Contributions from individuals or churches or church organizations will be received. Some churches will set a special goal for themselves in terms of a certain sum of money or of a certain piece of camp equipment. Two or three churches have indicated a desire to sponsor a cabin apiece. A brochure will be available, listing all camp buildings and furnishings needed, together with estimated prices.

February 11, 1951 has been named as Camp Sunday. On this day special offerings will be received in many churches. In other churches, where gifts have already been received, the day will be a day of dedication, in which reports on camping will be heard and prayers for camping will be offered.

PATHFINDER LODGE TO BE DEVELOPED

To serve the Baptist Churches of Eastern New York, Pathfinder Lodge has been developed. During the past summer a total of 400 Baptist young people have spent happy and helpful days on these Otsego shores. The site is beautiful beyond compare and all who spend a week there are thrilled with it.

Housing is still crowded and new tents and cabins are needed. An enlargement on the present Dining Hall is required to give greater facility in conducting a varied program.

Some individuals and churches will want to provide specifically for a cabin or a tent at this site.

Robert and Dorothy Vick, and their two sons set sail for their newly assigned mission field in Western China on December 15, 1946. Six weeks later their plane crashed near Hankow killing the father, mother and older son. Only 16-month-old Paul survived.

Letters from hundreds of friends soon indicated the tremendous impression that these young missionaries had made on the lives of young people they had led in Baptist camps. Many had taken a fresh look at the life of service and discipleship because of them.

It is most fitting that Bob and Dorothy, who made their decision for missionary service in camp and who gave their all for Christ should become a symbol of Baptist camping. Their names will be memorialized in the Western campsite.

Build Christian Character Through Camping

permanent dining hall was built and still stands today. Four tent areas were constructed on the other side of the lake, each with an outside cold-water trough and a primitive outhouse. A swimming area was created in the lake and a fleet of row boats and canoes obtained.

The lake was essentially a large pond created by a berm protecting it from runoff from a neighboring dairy farm as well as a concrete dam replacing a dam made by beavers. Portions of the lake were filled with lily pads, bulrushes, and other water plants through which there were channels to paddle a boat. The week was full of activities, ranging from crafts to discovery groups to vespers to bonfires at night. Many "camp romances" sprouted up, including one involving me. Over the years I have met many couples who first met at camp. Some of those couples went on to serve in the mission field and fill pastorates.

For several summers, my grandparents, Uncle George, and I spent a couple of weeks staying at my Aunt Bubbles and Uncle Earl's property in Webster while the Happ family vacationed at Lake Eaton in the Adirondack Mountains. My grandparents drove into Rochester each day for work while Uncle George and I stayed in Webster. This gave me free rein of the property, and I spent considerable time in the woods and orchards. I fondly remember plucking ripe peaches off the tree, lying in the grass and watching clouds roll by. We also picked fresh vegetables, including my favorite, sweet corn. Perhaps my best memory of my time in Webster was having the sleeping porch to myself. The cool night air, sounds of crickets and other night life emanating from the forest, including whippoorwills and owls, never failed to put me into a deep sleep.

Around 1954, the Happs decided to build a cottage on Lake Eaton in the middle of the Adirondack Mountains. They purchased land in a cove across from a public campsite where they had been staying for several years. A number of Uncle Earl's fellow employees at Eastman Kodak Company also purchased land, and soon cottages began to appear. Families, including twenty or so kids, began to stay the entire summer. The lake was relatively small (between five and ten miles in circumference), making it ideal for canoes, rowboats, and small motor boats. About 150 feet off shore from the Happ cottage, relatively flat rocks jutted out of the water with a two-foot submerged ledge extending out another ten feet, ending with a sheer drop of fifteen feet, perfect as a swimming destination. The cottage was located about a mile down a dirt road off the main roadway, adjacent to miles of state forests. I began to spend one to two weeks every summer at the cottage, boating, swimming, hiking, and hanging out with the other kids.

One summer, several of my cousins and I decided to build a tree house. There was a lumber yard a little over two miles from the cottage. With permission from the lumber yard, we literally dragged or carried scrap lumber to land located behind the cottage containing four large trees forming a square. A ladder

FROM LEFT *Paul with cousins Bob and Randy Henry at Fairhaven Beach on the shore of Lake Ontario, New York, in the summer 1954.*

was created by nailing two-by-six boards to a tree. The tree house was constructed about twenty feet off the ground. On our journeys back and forth to the lumber yard, we discovered a granary door in an old barn, a perfect size for the floor of the tree house, thus finding it a new home. To this day we don't know who owned the barn or whether the granary door was ever missed.

The cottage was relatively small, consisting basically of two bedrooms and a kitchen/living room, but it had a large screened-in porch. The kids slept in sleeping bags arranged on the porch floor, like peas in a pod. Aunt Bubbles often read us stories to settle us down at night. My favorite were the Uncle Wiggily books.

As I have looked back on these early years of my life, I have come to understand what a gift and blessing it was to have been surrounded by a loving and giving family, helping to build a foundation on which I could explore how to live the life given to me.

Chapter 14

My High School, College, and Graduate School Years

A major transition in my life occurred in the fall of 1958 when I entered eighth grade at Monroe High School. I went from being in a grade with about sixty pupils to one with more than 300. That first year I felt overwhelmed, and my grades showed it. By the end of the year, however, I had acclimated to the school, resulting in passing grades in all subjects. Although I was not much of a joiner, I participated in debate club and joined Beta Hi Y, becoming the treasurer (a role that seemed to stick for the rest of my life). During my junior and senior years, I ran track (the half mile) but looking back, I was most likely allowed to run in the meets because I had access to a car and could transport other members of the team. To my credit, I didn't always come in last.

During my high school years, much of my life was centered around the church, particularly with Baptist Youth Fellowship and Monroe Baptist Youth Fellowship. Every Sunday Grandpa and Grandma Vick made sure to arrive at church early to secure "Grandma Vick's seat," which was the last pew on the right facing the front of the church. Until junior high age, most of my involvement was through the Sunday school program and attending the dinners and other frequently held social gatherings. Church membership was close to 500, and every pew on the main floor and in the balcony was filled to capacity. Rev. Robert Slaughter, pastor of the church from 1954 to 1960, baptized me at Easter time in 1956. I became good friends with his older son, and together we found ways to get into mischief. During the service, we sat in the last pew in the balcony and shot spit balls, earning a scowl from the pulpit. We also explored the attic and bell tower, which could only be accessed by ladders through trap doors. We had to be careful navigating our way around the attic as the "floor" consisted of planks where one misstep could send us through the ceiling (a major fall especially over the sanctuary).

To the best of my recollection, there were twenty to twenty-five young people in the church youth fellowship program at Immanuel. We generally met on Sunday evenings at the church to socialize and discuss issues and concerns significant to us. We raised money by holding car washes, newspaper drives, and hiring ourselves out to church members to do cleanup and odd jobs. A major activity each year was the decorating of the church sanctuary for Christmas. Other church members and I have continued to this day the tradition of the "hanging of the greens."

My high school years came to an end with graduation in June 1963. That summer, Lee Flanders and I took a trip through Michigan, camping, hiking, canoeing, and visiting relatives. We travelled as far as north as Mackinac Island and down the eastern side of Lake Michigan. We also stopped by Kalamazoo College, which I would be entering that September. It was a special time with Lee that created lasting memories.

The remainder of the summer I worked in Grandpa Vick's insurance office in the Davis building on the corner of East Avenue and Gibbs Street. It was situated on the second floor with large plate glass windows overlooking East Avenue. Growing up, my cousins and I watched the

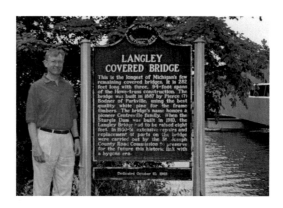

Paul next to a sign commemorating a covered bridge near a one-room school house attended by his grandfather Lester Flanders in Colon, Michigan. Photo taken at a family reunion around 1981.

annual Memorial Day parade with that vantage point providing an unobstructed viewing. Those windows were also a source of heat radiation. I recall days when the temperature in the office would be in the 90s with the only source of air movement being one floor fan. My primary job was to file fire rating cards for property, about as stimulating as watching moss grow. That summer experience was enough to settle for me the issue of whether I would go into the insurance business.

The summer of 1963 stands out for another reason: I bought my first car. The student minister at our church, whose parents had been missionaries in Burma, was selling his 1957 Volkswagen Beetle with a canvas sunroof. I purchased it for $400 and became quite popular. At one time we squeezed seven people into the car; two had to stand up with their heads sticking out of the top. When it came time to start college, Uncle Earl purchased it from me for the same price I had paid. Not a bad deal.

During that same summer, the World Council of Churches convened at Colgate Rochester Divinity School. A number of young people from local churches, including myself, became "chamber maids" making beds and cleaning rooms. One room we cleaned housed the Archbishop of Canterbury. His regalia and vestments were impressive. This was the first occasion I spent time in the Trevor/Eaton dormitories where my father had lived as a student. I gained an appreciation of what life must have been like when the school was overflowing with residential students.

OF THE THREE COLLEGES where I applied for admission (Denison University, my father's alma mater; Ottawa University, where three of my cousins went; and Kalamazoo College, an American Baptist institution), Kalamazoo was by far my first choice. Its size (approximately 1,200 students then), academic reputation, innovative year-round quarter system, foreign study program, and affordable cost combined to make this school a good fit. I was surprised to learn that ten of my classmates came from the Rochester area, partly due to a strong local alumni chapter. That first fall quarter was a challenge academically. I had not received a good foundation in writing nor had I been exposed to significant classical writers or poets. As it turned out, the course that had the most impact on my academic development—and the one where I received the worst grade ("D")—was freshman English. However, the class built a foundation that has lasted my lifetime.

That first year, my main extracurricular activity involved the freshman basketball team. In tryouts, it soon became clear that I did not have the skills to make the team, so I elected to become a manager. That meant that I could travel with the team for away games. The best part of those trips were the great meals we had on the way back to the school.

That first Thanksgiving away from home was also memorable. Great-Uncle Zoe Flanders and his wife, Zadie, picked me up at the college and drove me back to their home in Colon, Michigan, for Thanksgiving. Uncle Zoe had recently sold his farm (where I had stayed as a boy) and moved into town. Aunt Leatha (Grandpa Flanders' younger sister) and many of my cousins who lived within striking distance also gathered around the table for a good old-fashioned farm Thanksgiving. The food, as good as it was, paled to the experience of being with down-to-earth people, full of warmth and love, who fully embraced me as a part of their family.

Kalamazoo College operated on the quarter system, so we took our final exams before the Christmas break, which lasted for three weeks. At the end of that first quarter, all eleven of us from the Rochester area took the same train to Rochester. This was the era of hootenannies, and two of our members had amazing voices and played the guitar. We got the entire car involved in singing Bob Dylan, Pete Seager, and Peter, Paul and Mary songs. Interestingly, Kalamazoo was just 500 miles from Rochester, which gave special meaning to one of those songs.

That first break from college was a wild time. We often headed out to Tiny's Bengal Inn by Lake Ontario where the Invictas played (their song "The Hump" made the national charts). The place was always jammed, making it difficult to move around. The cigarette smoke was so dense that our eyes watered, and we had to escape outside periodically.

My winter and spring quarters at Kalamazoo College were uneventful. I had adjusted to college life, and my academics improved. I majored in history with political science as a minor. I also began to take courses in education in the event I decided to pursue a teaching career.

The summer of 1964 stands out because of the eruption of racial violence in the city of Rochester. When news of the uprising came over the radio, I was on Durand Beach on Lake Ontario with friends. Of course, a friend and I immediately drove downtown but found that police had blocked off the entire area around Joseph Avenue. We could see burning buildings and people looting stores. The uprising made national headlines. The Council of Churches immediately reached out to clergy and churches in the area seeking to calm the rage that had bubbled over. Eventually order was established, and efforts began to address causes that had given rise to the uprising.

Through the auspices of the Council of Churches, young people in and outside that area began to meet to search out ways of responding to the injustices experienced in a city of deep racial divide. I was asked to be a part of that group. The uprising paved the way for the creation of the organization FIGHT (Freedom, Independence, God, Honor, Today) and the bringing of Saul Alinsky to the city to take on the primary economic driver of the community, Eastman Kodak Company. The pastor of our church, Rev. Richard Brown, along with other pastors such as George Hill from Lake Avenue Baptist Church and Lee Baynon from First Baptist Church, joined forces with Herb White and Marv Chandler of the Council of Churches, who were the executive minister and associate executive minister respectively, to create the Friends of FIGHT to support efforts under way to provide greater opportunity for minority employment at Eastman Kodak as well as to improve housing within the impoverished areas of the city. William Vaughn, the president and CEO of Eastman Kodak Co and also a member of Immanuel Baptist Church, was supportive of the goals of FIGHT and opened channels of communication within Kodak. That resulted in training programs and employment opportunities demanded by FIGHT.

My main focus of my sophomore year was preparing for my career internship during the spring quarter and my foreign study during the fall and winter quarters of my junior year. I wasn't quite sure what career path I wanted to take but teaching, ministry, and law were primary areas of interest. I had attended high school with teens from the Hillside Children's Center, a residential facility for troubled youth, some of whom were placed there by the courts. I contacted the director for possible placement, and I became a group counselor, assisting in the residences and supervising recreational activities. This experience proved invaluable in building a foundation for work I undertook later while in seminary and beyond.

*　　　*　　　*

I spent the summer quarter on the Kalamazoo campus, focusing most of my energy on preparing to leave for France in August. Although I had taken French classes in high school and college, I had never become fluent enough to study in that language. My level of skill determined my placement, and I was assigned to attend the international school of the University of Aix-en-Provence, close to the French Riviera. Two classmates and I stayed with a family in the center of the city, about four blocks from the school, with four other students from Germany and England. The 300-year-old buildings on the block were all connected and fronted by a high wall that ran the length of the block. The three of us stayed in a second-floor large room with tall windows overlooking the street. The infrastructure of the city still felt the effects of the war, so water and heat had to be conserved. We were limited to two baths a week. The madame of the house needed to turn on the boiler to heat the water before we could take a bath.

The only meal we ate with Madame and her family (her husband, her adult son who lived at the house and periodically her adult daughter) was the evening meal. The specialty of every French meal is the soup served at the beginning. I will never forget my first meal with the family. When the soup was served, family members began to liberally sprinkle a "root extract" on the soup; they indicated it would enhance the taste. I followed their example. One spoonful later, I was gagging and tears were flowing. There was no water, only table wine, which I immediately grabbed and drained. Over time I became acclimated to this "taste enhancer" and used it every chance I had.

The university was about a 15-minute walk from where I lived. On my way to school in the morning, the aroma of freshly baked bread assailed me, making a lasting memory. All courses were on a pass/fail system, which minimized the stress of studying and allowed greater opportunity to absorb the culture. My classes were in French, international law, and art history. I don't remember much about the course work (probably because I missed a number of classes) but I do remember highways and byways of Aix-En-Provence, an ancient medieval city that once housed the Pope. I rented a scooter from time to time and rode throughout the countryside. I purchased food for meals at an open-air market in the center of the city. Staples consisted of eggs, flour, jam, bread, cheese, and wine. The eggs, flour, and jam were used to make crepes over a small burner we kept in our room. We also spent time at outdoor cafés where we could nurse a cup of coffee for a couple of hours supplemented by pastry.

During school breaks we traveled. Twice I took the train to Florence and Rome. I spent hours walking the streets and going to open-air markets, as well as visiting traditional tourist sites such as art galleries and historic locations. Perhaps my most memorable experience occurred at the Vatican when Pope Paul VI delivered his Christmas message. Entering St. Peter's Square, the Pope's car passed not more than twenty feet from me. At that time there was no protective covering over the car, so I got a close-up view of him as he rode by, waiving to the huge crowd.

I was fortunate to have a classmate who had traveled to Sweden to pick up a Volvo his father had purchased, which provided my friend with transportation while in Europe. One of the first trips we took in his Volvo was to Barcelona, Spain. To this day, I am amazed that we made it across the Pyrenees and back in the dead of winter without incident.

In February 1966, I returned to the United States by securing passage on the *Queen Elizabeth 2* ocean liner. Unfortunately, I had not considered the intensity of storms in the Atlantic during that time of year. As a consequence, I spent two of the five days on board in my bunk, miserable with seasickness. Fortunately, I recovered for the last two days. I was able to keep food down and I took advantage of many of the offerings available.

*　　　*　　　*

Upon my return, I became engaged to a girl I had grown up with in my home church of Immanuel. We had dated since my junior year in high school. While I was in Europe, we decided to get married. I returned to Rochester that fall to fulfill my student-teaching requirement at a middle school in Penfield while making plans for our wedding. We were married in December 1966 in Immanuel Baptist, and after a short honeymoon in the Adirondack Mountains, we returned to Kalamazoo for my last two quarters.

During the winter quarter, I struggled to decide on a career choice. I could return to Rochester where I was all but guaranteed a teaching position in the school in Penfield. I also was intrigued by the field of law and considered applying to law school. While taking an international law class in France, the analytical approach to problem solving resonated with me and created a curiosity to delve further into that field. In the end, however, I felt my heart pulling me toward divinity school. I applied and was accepted to the Colgate Rochester Divinity School. My wife and I moved back to Rochester and into married student housing on the school campus.

Paul graduated from Kalamazoo College in 1967 and then entered the seminary.

At that time, every seminarian was placed as a student minister with a church or in a non-traditional outreach program. My field assignment was outreach ministry with South Avenue Baptist Church under the mentorship of the pastor. I could not have been given a better assignment. Clergy in the area were seeking ways to engage their churches in an area of the city that was rapidly evolving from a white, blue-collar demographic to more multi-cultural. A seminary student from the Catholic seminary, Saint Bernard, and I were charged with going into the neighborhood called the South Wedge, which extended into the heart of urban Rochester. The area was economically impoverished and experiencing an increase in crime and gang violence. We began to connect with young people who had nowhere to go but the streets. We discovered some of them had put together bands but had no place to play. By the end of that first year, we had opened up several church basements and retrofitted them as coffee houses. The first to open was in the basement of South Avenue Baptist Church. Named "The Hangup," it was complete with black lights and large telephone wire spools as tables. Church members volunteered their time, and before long we had as many as 300 kids in attendance. Many of these kids were members of gangs. We had made it clear that all were welcome. The Hangup was to be considered neutral territory, a safe place to gather. As a security measure, we hired an off-duty police sergeant, whose nickname was "Doc" and who was known and respected by the kids, to be present whenever the coffee house was open.

Getting churches involved in opening their buildings to neighborhood kids and encouraging church members to become involved resulted in the formation of a coalition of churches located in the South Wedge.

Paul served as director of the Southeast Area Youth Ministry.
The group's efforts to provide a safe place for youths who had run
away from home were highlighted in The Times-Union newspaper.

As the number of churches involved grew beyond the South Wedge to include large metro churches along East Avenue, the focus expanded beyond youth to addressing the issues of poverty and exploitation of the vulnerable, especially the elderly and those suffering from mental health issues. Eventually seventeen churches formed the Southeast Ecumenical Ministry (SEM), which opened pathways for funding from not only churches but also church judicatories.

The Southeast Area Youth Ministry was formally organized as a part of SEM with a board populated by representatives from various churches. I was appointed as director with offices established in the rectory of Calvary St. Andrews Church in the South Wedge. By the end of my second year in seminary, we had established programs using the facilities of Third Presbyterian Church, Incarnate Word Lutheran Church, St. Paul's Episcopal Church, and Blessed Sacrament Church. We also built connections with Monroe High School and Hillside Children's Center as well as Monroe Avenue Co-op and the Center for Youth, resulting in a network that offered places where teens could gather rather than hang out on the streets.

IN 1969, OUR EFFORTS TO HELP alleviate family dysfunction and violence received a big boost when a coalition that included our youth ministry received a federal grant to bring mental health resources into the community. We were able to lease properties outside of the church as drop-in centers for youth, expand staff, and make available mental health support services from the Mental Health Department of Strong Memorial Hospital. These resources provided people in the community with tools allowing for constructive intervention in destructive behaviors experienced on a daily basis. We also obtained several Vista workers to supplement existing staff, and we developed a core community group of approximately sixty volunteers.

An article in the Family section of *The Times-Union* newspaper in Rochester featured our efforts to fix up the former Frick Funeral Home at South Avenue and Comfort Street. We were converting it into a place for runaways to stay. Among the photos is a headshot of me, at age 25, with a beard and mustache and hair long enough to touch my back collar. "This is one of the biggest needs in Rochester," I'm quoted as saying. "There are no places for runaways, and the only way a kid can really get into a shelter is to commit a crime. There are a lot of kids roaming the streets at night simply because they have no place to go."

In addition to my project work and even though I had not yet graduated from seminary, I became a supervisor for other seminarians who wanted to be placed in ecumenical field assignments. What had begun as a field placement for me had turned into a full-time job.

In the spring of 1969, two other events happened. My wife and I purchased a house at 360 Rockingham St. from an estate. Soon after, Grandpa Vick died. He was fully active up to a week before his death. His passing was a huge loss for me. From the time I had returned from China as a tiny boy, Grandpa Vick's nurturing soul, his love, and his support of me were constant and steadfast. In his own quiet way, Grandpa Vick had been a pillar of strength for me and had deeply influenced my life in ways that became increasingly clear as I lived into my own life experiences. He was a man of deep faith who taught by word and deed the sacred value of all whom we encounter and this creation that has been given us.

Because of my responsibilities overseeing the youth outreach project, I had to reduce my divinity school workload, which extended my studies an additional year. Although I was ordained by the Monroe Baptist Association in 1970, I didn't actually graduate until May 1971. It was toward the end of 1971 that three additional events happened that altered my life. Grandma Vick died in November, just shy of her 91st birthday. Grandma Vick, together with Aunt Bubbles and Aunt Carol, had provided the maternal nurturing for me during childhood and into my adult life. With her death, the three adults with whom I had lived — Uncle George and Grandpa and Grandma Vick—were gone, losses felt deeply by me. The second event was the joy of learning that my wife and I were about to have our first child, a beautiful daughter. I felt a deep regret that my fraternal grandparents had both died before they knew that their son would have been a grandparent.

The third event was my decision to go to law school. A number of attorneys who volunteered in the Youth Project encouraged me to consider the study of law as a means of broadening my effectiveness in community outreach. I took the LSAT exam during the fall of 1971 and was accepted into the New England School of Law in Boston. At the same time, friction developed between the Southeast Area Coalition (SEAC), a community organization that was my employer, and the direction the Youth Project was taking under my leadership. In February 1972, the SEAC board decided to fire me. That action set in motion a chain of events that ultimately ended in the demise of the Youth Project by the end of the year. Forces that were more concerned with maintenance of property values than with the conditions creating poverty and the plight of those in the community struggling to survive won out.

The six months between my termination as Youth Project director and my entering law school were some of the happiest months of my life up to that point. My wife and I had opened our house to four student boarders from Rochester Institute of Technology (we had four bedrooms on the second floor and had turned a finished attic into a fifth bedroom). I took on an interim pastor position with the York Baptist Church and began upholstering furniture in the basement of our house.

My wife and I also prepared for the birth of our daughter, taking childbirth classes and accumulating the necessary clothes and supplies. The original due date came and went. After the passing of an additional three weeks, my wife finally went into labor. We called the doctor and rushed to the hospital, which was only three blocks away; tire marks could be seen on the street for some time after. There was no air conditioning in the hospital, and we were in the midst of a heat wave. Finally the miracle and blessing of new life occurred. Our lives were forever changed. Our daughter, Jennifer, had taken her time coming, but after many hours of labor, I felt a joy I had not experienced in the past. Holding this new life in my arms and looking into her eyes, my heart was touched in a new and profound way .

Law school education represented a complete change from my work in seminary. Four of my courses were year-long, with the grade based on one exam at the end of the year. There was no way to know how well I was doing other than through classroom interaction. Our professors encouraged us to form study groups. There were four of us in my group and we began to click from the start. To break up the intensity and stress of study, we played bridge. By the time finals rolled around, we felt confident enough to continue our bridge playing in the student lounge while others were cramming for exams. I remember the professor who taught the contracts class stopped by the lounge. He noticed we were engaged in a serious game of bridge and commented that although the faculty encouraged students to relax, he thought we were carrying it to an extreme. All four of us ended in the top ten in our class of nearly 300. I was ranked fifth.

My grades were good enough that I applied to transfer to the University of Buffalo Law School as my ultimate goal was to practice in New York State.

To my delight, I was not only accepted but also received a New York State scholarship that paid my entire tuition. During the summer of 1973 we moved from Boston to an apartment off Niagara Falls Boulevard in Amherst about a mile from the law school. The law school had just moved from Eagle Street in downtown Buffalo into the first building built on the new campus in Amherst.

I couldn't have asked for a more accommodating child than Jennifer. When I needed to study in that first year of law school, she napped, and when I was able to spend time with her, she was ready to do things with me. When we moved to Amherst, we reluctantly decided to place Jennifer in the Mother Goose Daycare in North Tonawanda. This was a traumatic decision for us, as our daughter had always been in the care of one or of both of us. When I dropped Jennifer off at Mother Goose that first day, she just stood there looking at me with the "are you out of your mind" look. My heart was breaking, but I knew there was no alternative.

Perhaps my greatest surprise during this time was the direction my law courses were taking me. I had originally envisioned engaging in some type of public law. Instead, I found myself concentrating in the area of tax law and how our tax laws shaped and were an expression of societal values. Not wanting to work in government or the corporate sector, I knew that I needed to seek a position in private practice. Upon graduating in 1975, I was faced with taking the New York State Bar exam and then waiting to see if I passed; I had no job prospects waiting in the wings. I spent the summer studying and taking the exam.

Chapter 15

Raising a Family and Managing a Career

Somehow, I made it through the summer and landed a position with the firm Bonello, Gellman, Anton, Bridges, and Conti in Niagara Falls. After graduating, we moved to North Tonawanda, which meant a 20-minute drive across Grand Island and up the Robert Moses Expressway to get to work. The office was located close to the falls but the city itself had fallen on hard times. During the winter, I had to turn the car's heater and fan off because of the chemicals spewing from the chemical plants located along the expressway.

When I received word that I had passed the bar exam, we decided it was time to return to Rochester. One of the attorneys who had encouraged me to go to law school had just joined three other young attorneys forming a new firm. He paved the way for me to become an associate in a tight market for new attorneys. Through the assistance of contacts our firm had with a local lending institution, my wife and I were able to submit an offer to purchase a home in Rochester.

Financially we were tapped out, but we were able to close and move into the house before the birth of our second child, who was due to be born in June. The birth of our first son, Chris, was as much of a miracle to me as was the birth of Jennifer. However, Jennifer was not so sure having a brother was such a good idea. She had had us to herself for four years. Now her status was threatened by this "interloper," who commanded so much of our attention. We made sure that when people came to visit, they would also bring gifts for her and otherwise acknowledge her in special ways.

This was a challenging time for me. We now had the responsibility of two children, and I was trying to establish myself in the practice of law. Because of my church and denominational connections, I was asked to become a member of the board of trustees at Immanuel as well as a member of the regional board of the Monroe Baptist Association. The denomination had just re-organized, making our association one of thirty-four regions across the United States and Puerto Rico. I helped create our regional organizational structure, which required drafting new bylaws. I was asked to become the first president-elect, which meant that I would serve two years heading up the newly created program division with the president heading up the administrative division. We had no model to work from, so we were building something new. It was exciting but extremely time-consuming.

At the same time, a former volunteer in the Youth Project asked me to join the Monroe Association for the Hearing Impaired, underwritten by Hetti Shumway, a wealthy philanthropist in Rochester. My ministerial experience and legal expertise filled a needed role as they attempted to organize under the umbrella of the Monroe County Health Association.

In 1979, I was asked to provide legal representation for and go on the board of Alternatives for Battered Women. This organization was in its infancy and had just been licensed to open a shelter for abused women and their children in the old Jewish Y that had been acquired by the Freddie Thomas Foundation. For the first several years, much of my time focused on helping staff secure orders of protection on behalf of those in the shelter, by my bringing petitions in Family Court to quash subpoenas meant to intimidate those who had sought shelter with the agency. After the building was sold to a developer, I was forced to go to court to obtain an order of protection against the owner who had become threatening to staff and residents. This prompted a move to a new location with much greater security. Funding continued to expand to a point that when I left some seventeen years later, we had an annual operating budget of more than seven million dollars and had become a model agency for survivors of abuse throughout New York State.

On February 7, 1978, another blessing came into our lives with the birth of our second son, Ben. The day of delivery saw Rochester being hit with a ferocious winter storm that immobilized the city. I managed to flag down a snowplow, borrow a four-wheel drive auto from a neighbor, and follow the snowplow for about two miles to Highland Hospital. What a ride that was. For a third time I experienced the joy of looking into the eyes of this new miracle of life.

*   *   *

My law practice continued to build in the field of estate and trust taxation and business succession planning. I became involved in the Monroe County Bar Association, chairing the estate and trust section. I presented seminars for the local and state bar associations as well as for financial planners and their clients. As my reputation grew, other attorneys began to consult with me, and I found myself working on increasingly complex issues involving larger and larger wealth accumulations. My peers voted me to be included in the Best Lawyers of America and New York Super Lawyers publications.

In 1982, our firm merged with the largest law firm in Buffalo, which provided me with greater financial security and increased compensation. It was not lost on me that in some respects I had wandered far from the initial reason I had gone into law—to develop tools to better serve others. It was for this reason, much to the consternation of my partners, that I provided financial planning and other legal advice to clergy and others, either on a pro bono basis or a greatly reduced rate. I maintained (and still continue) a legal counseling program for students at RIT. I became legal counsel for our American Baptist Region, a position I held for nearly twenty-five years, again on a pro-bono basis. I aided in the establishment of Cameron Community Ministries, an organization serving a mainly Hispanic population, which has become an anchor for that community and is now recognized as a ministry of the American Baptist Home Mission Society.

I became involved with the Fairport Baptist Homes Caring Ministries Board and helped set up a foundation to provide support for different levels of care serving the aging and infirm. Several years after I left the foundation board, I was honored by the establishment of the Paul A. Vick Philanthropy Award, given annually to persons who had made unique contributions to the various caring ministries supported by the foundation. I also was invited to join the board of trustees of my alma mater,

Colgate Rochester Crozer Divinity School, and became chair of the finance committee as the school sought a sustainable pathway forward.

Throughout all these years, the one constant was my church family at Immanuel Baptist. Unfortunately for my children, IBC, like many urban churches, had an aging population with few young families and fewer children. Our children did not have the same experience as I and my father before me had with a strong robust children and youth program. I was thrilled when each, in their own time, asked to be baptized. I was blest to be able to baptize each in the same baptismal in which I, and before me my father, had been baptized.

Chapter 16

New Beginnings: The Family

My world was turned upside down in 1995 when my wife and I separated after nearly thirty years of marriage. We had grown up together in Immanuel, and there had been no doubt in my mind that we were in a committed lifetime relationship. My world became totally disoriented. Our two older children were away at college, and our youngest was still in high school and living at home. I knew I had to try my best to stay focused for the sake of our children (not always successfully) and maintain my responsibilities as partner in charge of the estate planning department of our office. My grounding came through my church family and my work within the denomination and not-for-profit organizations.

I also went into therapy, questioning my judgement and the underpinning of how I understood the world around me. My therapist encouraged me to attend a ten-week group therapy program involving others dealing with profound loss in their lives. After completing those sessions, I became involved with Neutral Ground, a self-help program led by group leaders and held in ten-week sessions. After attending a couple of sessions, I was asked to become a group leader and went through training.

Once a month, the group leaders met at one of our homes. My first meeting with the group leaders was held at my home. Again, it was an event that altered my life. After the meeting started, a woman dressed in workout clothes arrived. What immediately struck me was her vivacious energy and her flashing brown eyes. As she was leaving at the end of the meeting, we spoke briefly in the kitchen. I learned that her name was Joyce Scorza and that she was an English teacher in East Rochester. She had been involved with Neutral Ground for a number of years and hadn't attended these monthly sessions for some time but for some reason decided to come that evening. She expressed surprise that this was my first meeting and was hosting the group. Nothing further was said.

Several days later I received a call from Joyce wanting to know more about the next session I would be leading as she thought it might be helpful for a friend of hers. We spoke for over an hour. Joyce had a couple of tickets to see *Stomp*, the Broadway production, and she wanted to know if I had an interest in seeing it. I readily accepted the offer and thoroughly enjoyed the performance. About a month later I phoned Joyce to let her know I was going to Boston to watch my oldest son in a crewing race. I asked her if she would like to have lunch with me before I left. She agreed to meet me, and we very much enjoyed it. We then began to spend more time together. We decided to team up to lead group sessions at Neutral Ground on spiritual disciplines. This was a new offering and one that the leadership was hesitant to approve, believing there would be little interest. The session was, in fact, over-subscribed with many being turned away.

Over the next year our relationship continued to develop. In addition to teaching school, Joyce was a docent at the Seneca Park Zoo and was serving as a volunteer hospice chaplain with Lifetime Care. As different as our personalities were (Joyce being an extrovert, never hesitant to speak her mind, and me being an introvert, generally absorbing and reflecting before speaking), we connected on a spiritual level bringing to our relationship the richness of different cultural traditions. Joyce was raised in the Conservative Jewish tradition.

Unknown to both of us, our paths must have crossed early in our lives. Although Joyce attended a different high school than I, she dated the president of my high school class and hung out with many of the Student Council and football team members, including the president of Beta High Y for which I had served as treasurer. We attended the same dances in the YMCA gym. However, we agreed that the extrovert party girl and the introvert shy boy would have had little in common. We were like ships passing in the night.

What was more amazing, however, occurred when we realized we both had student taught in the same school in Penfield, at the same time. Although we ate on the same makeshift stage in the auditorium as the school building was under renovation, we had no recollection of each other. Another coincidence was that my supervising teacher was the brother-in-law of a friend who had participated in a joint venture with Joyce and her then husband when they built a tennis club. At the time of our student teaching, I was preparing for my wedding with my first wife, and Joyce was preparing to marry her first husband, perhaps the reason we had no recollection of each other.

This time we met when our journeys were on the same path, and our differences were seen as mutually enriching strengths. On November 28, 1998, Joyce and I were married in a service I wrote based on the covenant between God and Noah, under a huppah and with the traditional breaking of the glass. Joyce's cousin, who rented out vintage Rolls Royce cars, provided transportation for the wedding party on a day with unseasonably warm weather in the high 70s. We were overjoyed that my children agreed to stand with us under the huppah.

THE NEXT SEVERAL YEARS brought even more change in the life of our family. Each of the children married, and soon grandchildren started coming. Between 2000 and 2015, seven new miracles of life joined our family. Words cannot fully capture the joy I felt as I held each newborn grandchild. A special moment for me, however, was being asked to dedicate our first grandchild in the sanctuary of the East Penfield Baptist Church where my father had served as pastor. I also officiated in the dedication of two other grandchildren in Immanuel Baptist Church, the third generation to be dedicated in that church. I also co-officiated in the dedication of two other grandchildren in their parents' home church.

In 2002 we moved to our present home in Brighton, a suburb of Rochester. We soon turned our basement into a magical world for our grandchildren. We set up a craft/music room filled with games and toys for both boys and girls. On several occasions, our grandchildren put together musical performances, complete with drums, keyboard, and guitars. They charged admission fees for us to hear original scores they created.

During summer vacation, Joyce renamed the more extensive times we had with the grandchildren as "Bubbe and Poppa Camp," complete

Paul and granddaughter Emma Vick share a special moment while perched on a giant rope-made spider web in the Adirondack Mountains.

with T-shirts. We took day trips to places such as Corning Museum of Glass and Niagara Falls. Each summer we spent at least a week at the cottage on Lake Eaton. A high point was the treasure hunt. I hid clues around the lake in places named Black Beard's Cove, Skull Rock, Long John Silver's Lookout, Pirate's Swamp, Sunken Island, etc. Some clues could be accessed by land, others only by boat. We all donned pirate head scarfs and eye patches and headed off to find the treasure, which at times was buried deep in the forest and other times could be found high in the trees. Red or black tape spelling "Beware" or "Danger" guarded each clue. As the grandchildren became older, friends were invited to stay with us at the cottage and were inaugurated into the pirate hunt experience, creating lasting memories.

The year 2015 came filled with great joy but ended in unspeakable tragedy. In May, our youngest grandchild, Charlie, was born. His two older sisters, Grace and Emma, now had a brother and were our three youngest grandchildren. Each of my grandchildren is a gift in my life and occupies a special place in my heart.

Emma's gift was making the most out of each moment of her life with unbridled joy and passion. From the time of her birth, I felt a unique bond forged with her. Whenever she saw me, her face instantly lit up and she ran to me screaming "Poppa" and jumped into my arms. When we went places, she reached for my hand and said, "Come, Poppa." She was in constant motion, rarely walking, and mostly running. She was full of life, finding joy in anything she did. One of the few times she stayed still was early in the morning. For three months in early 2015, Emma and her family stayed with Joyce and me while their house was being built. Emma, who was then 2 years old, and I were the early risers, and we developed a routine. I would open the door and find her standing in her crib. She would reach out her arms saying, "Poppa." I would take her out and sit in the rocking chair where she would nestle against me in the quiet of the morning. I would thank God that we were able to have that time together. When her younger brother was born, Emma became extremely protective of him, always checking on him to make sure he was all right.

That summer, our children and grandchildren spent time with Joyce and me at the cottage. For the first time, all of our grandchildren (including Avery, our only grandchild not to live near us), had the chance to go together on the pirate treasure hunt in full regalia. We also toured the Wild Center in Tupper Lake, an indoor/outdoor museum featuring animal, fish, and plant life indigenous to the Adirondack Mountains. There is an extensive display built into the trees with connecting bridges. One display is of a giant rope-made spider web. Emma was the only one who wanted to go down to the center of the spider web, so she grabbed my hand and led me to the center, a moment forever etched into my heart. We just sat there, side by side, with her hand on my leg, staring through the tree tops of the surrounding forest.

In December 2015, this hyperactive, loving child slipped away in her sleep from unknown causes, shattering all of our hearts. There is not a day that goes by that I don't think of our "wild one" and how she changed my life.

The Vick family. STANDING FROM LEFT *Jon, Jennifer, Aiden, and Jack Lazenby; Ben and Katherine Vick.* MIDDLE ROW FROM LEFT *Melinda Lazenby; Paul and Joyce Vick; Danielle, Chris, and Avery Vick.* FRONT ROW *Grace and Charlie Vick.*

Chapter 17

Following My Heart

As far back as I can remember, one way or another, some aspect of my life involved denominational and ecumenical church life, but never beyond the regional level.

Then, in 2006, the executive minister of our region asked my permission to submit my name to become a national representative on the American Baptist Churches (ABC) General Board. I knew that there was no way I could meet the responsibilities of managing a department within my 180-attorney law firm and take on this new role. As I thought and prayed about this decision, the realization hit me that by serving on the General Board, under the structure then in existence, I would also be placed on either the Home Mission Board or on the Board of the American Baptist Foreign Mission Society, also known as International Ministries (IM). In all my years up to that point in time, I had given little thought to involvement in IM other than as the sending organization of my parents. Something deep inside me stirred, and I knew what my answer would be. I would accept the invitation, conditioned on my appointment to the IM board and retire from my law practice. In my heart, I felt God had been preparing me for this moment, and I could not turn away from this call.

As was the case with most mainline denominations, International Ministries was challenged with decreasing denominational giving, requiring a change in its funding model from central support to personalized support of our missionaries. This created significant stress for our missionaries now tasked with raising a part of their support in addition to serving in the field. Then the Great Recession hit, just as I came onto the board. That resulted in a significant reduction in home staff and diminishing our endowment to a perilously low level. In 2009, the assistant treasurer was asked to resign, followed by our treasurer/CFO's resignation in 2011. The entire finance department had to be restructured.

At the same time, the ABC denomination was undergoing significant changes. The old board structure, based on regional representation, did not allow the boards to adequately fulfill their respective governing responsibilities, necessitating "unlinking" and reducing the size of the boards. Further, the national headquarters in Valley Forge, which had been built to house more than 700 people, no longer met the needs of IM and its national partners, requiring sale and relocation of offices.

My years of involvement with governance and resource management of not-for-profit organizations paved the way for my involvement in responding to these challenges. The position of treasurer of IM became a board position, which I was asked to take on. I worked with staff redesigning the operational structure of IM, including creating the position of comptroller and associate executive director for operations, to rebuild capacity to manage growing mission work. I became involved with an advisory group representing IM in the disposition of the home office property in Valley Forge, which turned into a ten-year project. I was also invited to serve on the finance committee of the American Baptist Churches USA, responsible for allocating the national portion of funds raised through denomination-wide United Mission giving.

*   *   *

My role as treasurer led to a totally unexpected involvement in the mission field in India. IM missionaries first arrived in India in 1835 when India was under British rule. During the ensuing 120-plus years, IM acquired substantial property throughout southern, eastern and northeastern India, establishing schools, hospitals, seminaries, and churches. When India gained its independence, legislators passed a law that required all foreign persons and organizations to divest their interest in the properties. In 1972, IM created a trust to take title to the property through a process referred to as an "amalgamation." Over the years, those in charge of the trust began converting property for personal use and benefit. IM's attempts to preserve the property with an estimated market value in the billions of dollars for missionary purposes resulted in extensive legal proceedings and caused friction and mistrust—sometimes with parties turning violent—among churches and others claiming relationship with IM. Overlaying the right to control the property was uncovering the fact that the agreement of amalgamation that had been approved by the courts had never been registered with the appropriate governmental authorities.

In 2012, Rev. Dr. Benjamin S. L. Chan, IM area director for East and South Asia, asked me to get directly involved in working toward resolution of the property issues that were a cause of anger and tension within the Christian Indian communities. In conjunction with Ben, an advisory group, of which I was a member, began to build an infrastructure to address not only property issues but also relational issues. I began to travel to India to assist in the building of new organizational structures while also building relationships by participating in mass celebrations and annual gatherings, significant church anniversaries, and new church dedications, often being asked to preach and bring words of encouragement and support. I could clearly see and feel God at work, as our partners in India, from the northeast to the south, began to join together to address critical issues confronting the church and the communities surrounding these churches. Such fellowship among peoples of different cultures, languages, and traditions would have been unimaginable, even a few years ago.

One of those significant developments was the creation of the India Mission Coordinating Committee (IMCC) designed to bring together Baptists from all over India. A first-ever summit was held in Kohima, Nagaland in the fall of 2014. The vision was to bring together people who were culturally diverse with deeply embedded mistrust of one another. Thousands attended, pledging to work together on issues of human trafficking, religious liberty, women in the church, and youth. The commissions and forums formed for each area of concern were to report back to a second summit to be held in five years in Hyderabad in Andrea Pradesh. In October 2019, more than 1,500 persons representing five million Baptists throughout India joined together in Hyderabad, representing the first time that ethnically and culturally diverse Baptists from across India were able to worship and celebrate together.

I had been asked to preach during a Sunday morning service at the Baptist Church Hyderabad, which has a sanctuary holding 8,000 people, and satellite churches with a combined membership of around 20,000. As I approached the church, I saw, to my amazement, a large plaque honoring Tracy Gibson, my father's classmate whom my parents met in San Francisco prior to sailing to China. In 1947, Tracy was commissioned as an American Baptist missionary to serve and work among the Banjara people (gypsies who are some of the most oppressed people in India). He assisted in the establishment of the church in Hyderabad as well as in providing educational opportunities and health care for the Banjara, which had been denied them. When I told church members of the connection between my family and Tracy, the community fully embraced me. I heard many powerful stories of how Tracy touched the lives of many. My opportunity to preach in this church could only have come about by the hand of God.

Joyce and Paul Vick ride on a cart pulled by bullocks in a parade through a village in a remote area of Andre Pradesh, India, in 2013. The parade led to a ceremony laying the cornerstone of a new church.

In 2014, Paul and Joyce Vick attended the first summit of all Indian partners of International Ministries held in Kohima, the capital of Nagaland, India. ABOVE LEFT *Joyce makes friends with local school children.* ABOVE *Paul participates in a group discussion during a breakout session of the summit, which was designed to bring together people of diverse cultures to work on a variety of issues.* LEFT *Paul with a member of the Naga tribes.*

AS MUCH AS MY LEGAL TRAINING and background had prepared me for this call in my life, a question raised by Reid Trulson, then IM executive director, surprised me. During an executive committee meeting in his home in November 2009, I was asked to share the story of my parent's call to the mission field. Afterward Reid asked me if I had considered going back to China. I had not given much thought to that possibility. I had no connections with China other than the stories my family had shared with me about my parents' call to serve in China, the plane crash and my rescue, and my return to my family in the United States. I knew we had departed from San Francisco aboard a converted troop ship, had landed in Shanghai where we stayed while waiting for transportation to Chengdu, had visited friends Gordon and Jean Gilbert in Hangchow, and that my parents and brother were buried in a cemetery in Hankow.

Reid's question awakened into my consciousness questions that I had never pondered; questions that perhaps had been lingering in my subconscious for years. What caused my parents to take a perilous journey to a war-torn country, exposing themselves and their two young children to so great a risk? What impact did their lives, and the lives of so many others called to serve during one of the most turbulent periods in China's history, have on the China of today? My response to Reid's question resulted in me giving a resounding yes to returning to China.

I started preparing for the trip by cataloguing volumes of letters, newspaper articles, publications, writings, communications from people who knew my parents, and other records created by my parents' families as well as their own writings. I traveled to Mercer College in Atlanta, Georgia, and spent several days going through archives of the American Baptist Historical Society. At the same time and totally unexpectedly, others who had had some connection with my parents and/or the crash began contacting me.

An organization formed by pilots who had flown for the China National Aviation Corporation (CNAC) located me to inquire if I was the sole survivor of the January 28, 1947 crash. The pilots invited Joyce and me to attend the annual meeting in San Francisco. We attended the reunion and met not only pilots who knew Red Holmes (who had flown me out of the crash site and had written to me an account of that experience) but also Capt. John Papajik who piloted the plane. These pilots' firsthand accounts of the dangers and challenges of flying in those early years of commercial aviation, especially in underdeveloped China of the mid-1940s, provided me with greater understanding of how risky had been the decision made by my parents to fly.

A friend contacted me about an amazing experience he had had while in China. He met a woman who had grown up in the St. Christopher's Orphanage in Hong Kong but now lived in California. She had been on a quest to discover her roots; she had tracked down a missionary now living in Toronto who had run the orphanage. She had been given a book written by that missionary's granddaughter. The book described a plane crash that had taken the life of the author's great-grandmother, Beatrice Kitchen. The book mentioned that there had been a sole survivor, a young child. My friend instantly

Paul with Tom Moore Jr. at the annual reunion of CNAC pilots in San Francisco in 2009. Moore, whose uncle was a CNAC pilot, is editor of the CNAC Historical website.

recognized that child was me. He put me in touch with the woman he had met, who in turn put me in touch with Muriel Tonge, the daughter of Beatrice Kitchen. Muriel had founded and run the orphanage. Muriel was now in her 90s. I connected with her and learned much of her family story, some of which I have incorporated into Part One of this book.

Frank Meller stands among the graves of his wife and children killed in the plane crash and at the head of Robert Vick's grave after their burial in China.

About the same time, Lynn Garth, the son of Bishop Schuyler Garth, traced me to Rochester and asked if we could meet. In spending time together, more parts of the story began to fall into place. I had earlier come across lengthy letters between my Vick grandparents and Frank Meller, whose wife and three children had also perished in the crash. These gave me further understanding of the other missionary family on that plane.

*   *   *

I began planning with Ben Chan of IM my return to China. Through his extensive contacts with the China Christian Council, we began to form an itinerary allowing us to retrace the places my family went while in China. In October 2011, Ben accompanied Joyce and me to China, landing in Beijing. We attended worship services and met with leaders of the local seminary. We then went to Nanjing to visit leaders of the Amity Foundation as well as with Judy Sutterlin, one of our missionaries, who was on the faculty of the national seminary. Her parents had been commissioned to serve in China the same time as my parents.

Ben Chan, right, International Ministries area director for East and South Asia, with Paul in Shanghai in 2011. Chan was instrumental in making contacts and planning the trip's itinerary.

She had been born in China, and her family was forced to leave when the communists took over. I had met her years before when she was pastoring a small church in the Rochester region. In the mid-1990s, she felt called to return to China after being invited by the Amity Foundation. She subsequently joined the faculty of the seminary.

From Nanjing, we traveled by train to Shanghai to meet with leaders of the National Office of the China Christian Council. They directed us to the church where my parents had worshipped during their time in Shanghai. We learned the location not only of the Blackstone Apartments where my family had stayed but also of the Country Hospital where I had recovered after the crash. We walked to the apartments from the church. The apartments appeared little changed from the time we had lived there. Even a plaque on the building still read "Blackstone Apartments." It was a strange experience to be standing on the same steps that my parents, Teddy, and I must have climbed those many years ago.

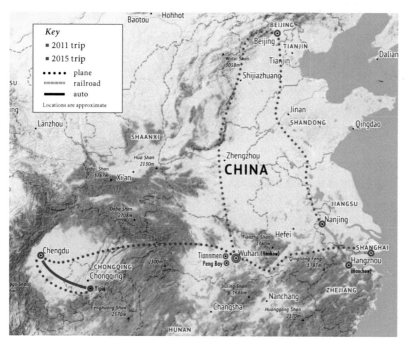

The route of Paul Vick's two return trips to China since he left after the crash in April 1947. In 2015, he traveled to Yipin, where his parents were to have ministered.

LEFT *Paul and Ben Chan at a meeting with the president and dean of Yanjing Theological Seminary in Beijing.* RIGHT *Ben, Paul, and Joyce visit with a staffer of the Amity Foundation in front of Amity Printing Co., which is the largest printer of Bibles in the world.*

A sprawling medical complex now surrounded Country Hospital. The building was little changed from the time I was there with extensive gardens and walkways. When we approached the building, security guards stopped us. Apparently, this building now provided care for government officials and other dignitaries. Ben tracked down the head of security and explained why we wanted to go inside. He relented to the extent of allowing us access to the ground floor only as well as to the gardens but photographs were not permitted. We surreptitiously took a few photos of the grounds.

Before leaving Shanghai, we toured the University of Shanghai for Science and Technology, which had been established by American Baptists and Southern Baptists in 1906. My father and mother had written about being taken to areas of the university that had been used by the Japanese to torture prisoners, and how painful it was for my parents to think of how those buildings had been transformed from chambers of learning into chambers of evil and suffering. We also visited the museum the University had built to preserve its history that included the role American Baptists had played during the first forty-five years of its existence. That university is now one of the largest in Shanghai. Many of the buildings in existence when we were there in 1947 still exist, including the chapel.

The next stop was Hangchow, where my family had stayed for a few days with Gordon and Jean Gilbert, who had traveled to China the preceding summer to serve the Wayland Academy, a school for elementary and high school students. Gordon Gilbert was another classmate of

LEFT *Joyce, Paul, and Ben in front of the former Yanjing seminary.* RIGHT *One of the original buildings of the Wayland Academy, where Gordon and Jean Gilbert, missionaries and friends of the Vicks, had served.*

my father's at CRDS. In later years, he was called to pastor Calvary Baptist Church in Rochester. When that church had to close, the proceeds funded an endowment with American Baptist Churches Rochester/Genesee Region to support equally domestic and foreign missions. The Wayland Academy is now one of the premier junior high schools in the city. We saw plaques telling the story of how the American Baptists founded the school. We also toured West Lake, which at one time had been the retreat for Mao Tse-tung; my parents had visited there and had described it in letters sent home.

The final leg of this trip took us to Wuhan (made up of three cities, including Hankow) where my parents and brother, along with the other missionaries and families who had died in the crash, were buried. While an investigation by members of the China Christian Council in Hubei Province and the Zhong Nan Theological Seminary were unable to identify the location of the cemetery, they were able to locate the place where the plane crashed.

THE RURAL VILLAGE OF PENG BAY was located approximately fifteen miles from the city of Tianmen and ninety miles west of Wuhan. Accessible only by a raft pulled across the Peng River by physically pulling on a rope running through pulleys, the village remained much as it was when the plane crashed. Upon arrival, the villagers were waiting for us as we walked up from the river. There were people who remembered

CLOCKWISE FROM TOP *Cotton still grows in the field where the plane crashed in 1947. Farmers in Peng Bay village excitedly tell Paul details about the day of the plane crash and their efforts to put out the fire. Joyce and Paul with Zhang Shuilian, a seminary professor, in front of the river where the plane's left wing fell.*

the crash and the baby who had been taken from the site of the burning wreckage. While the story they shared and that I tell in Chapter 2 of this book filled in more gaps in my story, it wasn't until I stepped onto the field where the burning plane had crashed, that the significance of where I was standing struck me to my core. I was standing in a cotton field, unchanged from how it looked as the burning fuselage was falling from the sky about to hit the ploughed field. It had been and remained a quiet pastoral scene interrupted by great tragedy.

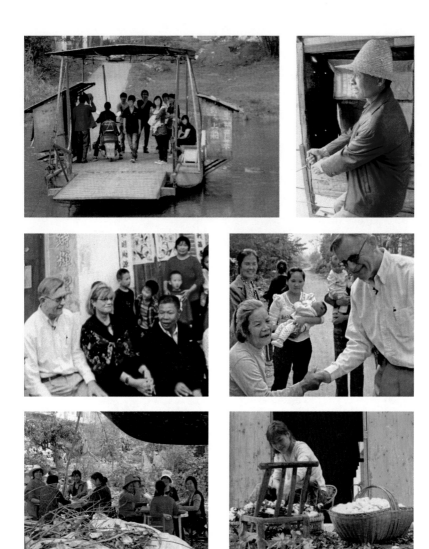

CLOCKWISE FROM TOP LEFT *Just as in 1947, a small ferry is still being used in 2011 to bring people across the Peng River to reach the village of Peng Bay.* TOP RIGHT *The captain maneuvers the ferry. Paul meets the woman who as a young girl had witnessed the plane crash and went for help. A woman cards the picked cotton to remove debris. The women of Peng Bay gather in this community spot to eat lunch or work on various projects together. Paul and Joyce talk with the son of the woman who nursed toddler Paul.*

During the Cultural Revolution from 1966 to 1976, all religion was outlawed. Zhang Shuilian, one of the professors at the Zhong Nan Theological Seminary, had explained to us that one way that Believers could share their love of Christ was by committing scripture to song to be sung in small home gatherings. This connection to scripture was a source of comfort and strength. As Joyce and I departed from the site of the crash, she began to sing to me, "Jesus loves me this I know."

Upon returning to the village, the families of that village gathered around me and gave me a new name—Peng Bao Lo (Paul of Peng Bay). The families of that village had taken me in as a member of their village and a part of their family.

Finding the cotton field was a meaningful discovery on its own, but standing in it and meeting the villagers only deepened my question: "Why did my parents feel called to come to this remote area of China?"

The entire village of Peng Bay turns out to welcome Paul and Joyce Vick. It was Paul's first visit since the plane crash.

During Paul's visit, the families of Peng Bay show their affinity to him by bestowing on him the name Peng Bao Lo, which means Paul of Peng Bay.

彭保羅

Chapter 18

The Completion of a Mission

In 2015, Joyce and I returned to Wuhan, accompanied by Rev. David Wong, special assistant to Ben Chan. As important as the first trip had been, I wanted a deeper understanding of the area my parents had been called to serve. International Ministries had had no contact with West China since the communist takeover. I felt a strong calling to complete the trip my parents were unable to complete.

A few weeks before we were scheduled to return to China, friends in Wuhan notified us that gravestones had been unearthed at an excavation site in the general vicinity where it was believed the International Cemetery had been located. Further research had confirmed that my family's gravestone had been a part of the cemetery.

We arranged to meet with people who knew of the cemetery before it had been destroyed, which most likely happened during the Cultural Revolution. With the aid of photographs, landmarks, and archival records that we discovered had been maintained in a nearby registration office, we found the approximate location of my parents' and brother's graves. However, no remains were discovered in the excavation site, and no records could be located indicating what may have happened to those remains. Local residents recounted how they had played in the cemetery when children. They called it the "big garden." I liked that; it made me glad that this place, which could be filled with much sadness, had brought joy to children. One of the residents recalled my family's tombstone as it was so different from the others.

Finding the gravesite of my family means more to me than I can say. It's customary for missionaries who die abroad to be buried there, with the idea that this is the country to which God called them. They symbolically become a part of the soil, to give birth to new life, to nurture seeds that their lives represented in the spread of the Gospel in China.

From Wuhan, we traveled to Chengdu where my parents were to have studied Chinese at Hua Xi BA (West China Union University) before heading on to their ultimate destination in Yipin. Founded by five mainline denominations including ABFMS and now a part of XiChuan University, the school has grown into the largest medical school in China. We met Dr. Zhang LiPing, who had written a book on the origins of the university and the role of Christian missionaries in the development of West China. She spent a day and a half taking us through the original buildings constructed by the mission societies, which are still in use today. As we discovered elsewhere, the Chinese preserve their history and have maintained this part of the campus much as it was seventy-four years ago, including an auditorium where a memorial service was held for the missionaries who died in the airplane crash.

VISITING THE UNIVERSITY made me feel that I was, in a sense, fulfilling the journey that my parents had been on. As I stood in the auditorium, I felt as though I was standing on sacred ground. Even though my parents never set foot on campus, I believe their spirit resides there and continues to inspire. As we prepared to leave the campus, we saw some students taking graduation photos. I couldn't help but

Paul and Joyce with a group of recently graduated students from the largest medical school in China, part of XiChuan University in Chengdu. Paul's parents had planned to study Chinese there when it was known as West China Union University.

think of my parents. I could easily envision my parents there, so happy and proud to have studied at this university.

As we were touring the campus, we came upon a group of young people who had just graduated. In seeing the young, eager faces of these graduates, and in talking to some about their future plans, I could see why my parents had given up so much to come here. Like young people all over the world, in every era, the challenges to overcome to reach their dreams just don't seem important.

We next travelled to Yipin, located approximately halfway between Chengdu and Kunming. I was anxious to get there; Yipin was the place where my parents were to have served and I was to have lived there. I hoped that finally seeing it in person would bring me full circle. Situated at the convergence of three major rivers in China (one of which is the Yangtze River, which flows across China to Shanghai), it once was the cultural and economic capital of the region. Missionaries first arrived in the late 1880s and began to establish schools and hospitals in addition to churches. Hostility and mistrust of the missionaries, combined with almost constant warfare, often led to persecution and sometimes death. At times when the danger peaked, the missionaries would leave temporarily, but they always returned with more people and stronger missionary work than before, spreading beyond Yipin.

By the time my parents were commissioned to serve in Yipin, six schools, a nursing school, and two hospitals had been established by

Joyce and Paul Vick, left, and David and Kathy Wong, right, with the medical director and senior administrative staff of the third largest hospital in West China. International Ministries established the hospital in 1889 in Yipin.

missionaries. My mother, as a trained nurse, was to have served in the hospital, while my father was to support outreach to more than forty communities surrounding Yipin, in addition to working with farmers to improve agricultural production.

Soon after the plane crash that killed my parents, the Chinese government (now run by communists) expelled all missionaries from around the country. International Ministries had had no contact with this region of China for more than sixty years. On arriving in Yipin, we did not know what to expect. To our surprise and delight, we found that the institutions established by ABFMS, including the church, were thriving. The hospital had become the third largest hospital in West China. The schools had been combined into one institution, now on two campuses with more than 4,000 students. The role of ABFMS in helping to create

ABOVE *Paul and Joyce Vick, center front row, and David and Kathy Wong, at left, visit a satellite chapel in a rural village outside Yipin in 2015.* LEFT *Paul with other church members at a site planned for a new church.*

Visiting Yipin, where Paul's parents were to have served as missionaries, and meeting the congregation of a satellite chapel in a rural village nearby helped Paul to understand his parents' calling. Seated from left are Stanley Chow, a videographer from Hong Kong who accompanied the Vicks; Joyce and Paul Vick, and David and Kathy Wong. David Wong is special assistant to Ben Chan, International Ministries area director for East and South Asia.

these institutions had been carefully preserved and displayed in murals on buildings for all to see. The missionaries established a model of a central church in Yipin providing pastoral support for outlying communities, and we found that continues firmly in place.

After attending a church service in Yipin where I spoke about my parents, our hosts took us to a smaller gathering in a nearby community. Each Sunday, two of the pastors from this church visit a community in the region to preach and teach the people about Christianity.

Seeing this in person brought many things to light for me. I could see how the earliest missionaries sacrificed and worked hard to make connections and reach people in need in whatever way they could. I could also see how my parents would have fit into the community here and how glad they would have been to make those connections.

The short time with these people was filled with joy and enthusiasm. It's truly a wonder what God can do in the hearts of women, children, and men when they begin to know and understand the love God has for them.

This trip provided a tremendous revelation to me. I now understood why my parents had been called to become missionaries.

Today, there are more than 100 million Christians in China. New churches are being planted at such a rate that it creates a major challenge to provide trained pastoral leadership. The seminaries are filled to capacity, with size limited only by available faculty. The Amity Foundation has printed more than 200 million Bibles in a printing plant funded in part by the Chinese government. Throughout our travels, we saw seeds, planted by missionaries and which the Cultural Revolution had sought to eradicate, springing to new life. The Cultural Revolution could not snuff out the fires that burned in the hearts of those whose lives had been transformed by the reassuring message of God's love for His creation. A video entitled *The Vineyard* features these two trips to China and can be seen on YouTube, https://www.youtube.com/watch?v=3NEjfKMZxuEf.

Chapter 19

The Beginning of the
Next Chapter

In 2012, members of the Zhong Nan Theological Seminary in Wuhan, whom we had first met during our visit in 2011, were invited to attend the International Ministries World Mission Conference held on American Baptist Conference grounds in Green Lake, Wisconsin. While in the United States, they stayed at our home in Rochester for several days during which time I arranged a meeting with faculty and administration at the seminary, now known as Colgate Rochester Crozer Divinity School (CRCDS). Understanding the need for enhanced education for faculties teaching in Chinese seminaries, and the historical role CRCDS played in responding to that need, I saw an opportunity to explore a possible relationship between our two seminaries.

Although that opportunity was not pursued, interest in cross-cultural education has resurfaced with the calling of a new president, Dr. Angela Sims, and the addition of a new faculty member, Dr. Jin Young Choi. Both have expressed interest in accompanying me to Northeast India to engage with theological educators. We planned a trip for April 2020 but postponed it due to the outbreak of Covid-19. However, we've connected with the principal of Eastern Theological College (ETS) in Johart, Assam, one of the largest and oldest seminaries in India. Plans are underway to travel to India in 2021 or 2022 under the auspices of International

Ministries. It is exciting to think of what might result out of collaboration between these two institutions having the same goal, the preparation of men and women as ambassadors of the Gospel message. (As a side note, on one of our trips to India, Joyce and I stayed at that seminary. We learned of the role IM missionary Rev. Dr. Frederick Downs played as a faculty member. Dr. Downs had a personal relationship with my home church, Immanuel. Recently I uncovered communications between the church and Dr. Downs indicating the church had raised nearly $30,000 to help renovate and expand ETC more than fifty years ago.)

My involvement with CRCDS was resurrected when I was asked to return to the board of trustees to chair again the finance committee. The school has been in transition over the last few years. Facing the reality of no longer being a residential seminary, the campus was sold and a new campus established in the heart of Rochester. New personnel were hired who shared the understanding of the role of theological education within the framework of a society and culture that had been undergoing major transition. Financial resources that had been consumed with the maintenance of a campus would now be deployed toward creating avenues of engagement within the Rochester community and beyond while maintaining the core values of education that is pastoral, prophetic, and learned.

I continue my role as treasurer of International Ministries. With more than a hundred global servants and partnerships in more than seventy countries, the challenges of supporting a seventeen-million-dollar budget are significant. Working with those who have been called to serve is both humbling and inspirational. New doors are constantly being opened, and I look forward to each new chapter in the life of this more than 205-year-old mission organization in which I have been blest to play a small part.

My FAMILY IS ALSO UNDERGOING TRANSITION. Our oldest grandson is in his second year in college. This year, our next oldest grandchild also will head off to college. Our youngest grandchild is now in first grade. As this next generation grows up and follows his or her own path, I can't help but wonder what world each will encounter and how each will use the gifts that God has given him or her to help bring this creation of His closer to the creation He would have it be.

The family I was born into were people of strong faith and conviction. They lived their faith with integrity and instilled in each succeeding generation an understanding of personal responsibility and accountability. They valued hard work and trusted that their labors would yield benefit not only for themselves and their families but also the wider communities in which they lived. Emotions of anger and indignation arose in the face of injustice and actions that caused harm to others. Throughout, there was a deep-rooted belief in a God of love and a simple trust that God was ever-present in their lives. At a young age, my father's heart was opened to God's presence in his life, which resulted in his burning passion to open the hearts of others to that love. When missionaries serving in China made known to him the conditions of poverty, suffering, and injustices afflicting so many lives, my father knew a path had been set before him that he must travel. He met a partner, my mother, who felt God's call to join him on that path.

When I share the story of my family, the question often arises as to why bad things happen to good people. For me, that came to be the wrong question. For me, the question is what was the impact of the lives my parents lived. Their lives have touched and inspired the lives of others. Through their lives, seeds have been planted that continue to bear fruit, fruit that will abide.

As mentioned previously, the American Baptist Foreign Mission Society published in 1947 a booklet about my parents entitled *The Worth of a Life*. In that booklet is written, "The worth of a life is not to be measured by its length but by the warmth of devotion and the quality of its service to a great cause." It is also written that "It is not a tragedy to die young. It is a tragedy to go through life and not know what life is really for." Those words of wisdom have helped guide me on the path that has been set before me.

Reflections

Pictures of my parents hung front and center in the front room of 142 Harvard St. over a table that displayed more framed photos of my parents. Some members of my family referred to this display as "The Shrine." The church and schools I attended, the area where I lived, the people with whom we associated were the same places and people with whom one or both of my parents had previously been involved. Although Grandpa and Grandma Vick tried to not place a burden of expectation on me, it was always there in the ways in which I was treated and viewed. I lived to a certain extent in the shadow of my parents. In a way, I felt that I was being measured and evaluated within the context of who they were. A high bar had been set by what many saw as my parents' martyrdom.

My grandparents often took me to churches where my father had preached for special occasions, such as Atlantic Avenue Baptist Church and East Penfield Baptist Church. Many knew my parents (as well as my brother and me) before the plane crash, and my parents had made an impression on them. When I was 12 years old, a Baptist summer camp was dedicated to the memory of my father, mother, and brother. Camp Vick, as it was dedicated, was located on 240 acres in the southern tier of New York State. Both of my grandfathers and I planted a tree in my parents' memory in a ceremony witnessed by more than a hundred people. When I attended Camp Vick as child, inevitably the story of the plane crash and my survival was told. It sent shivers up and down my back.

LEFT *Paul was very active in Immanuel Baptist Church growing up, including singing in the choir. He stands in front of photos of his deceased parents that were displayed prominently in his grandparents' home.* RIGHT *Paul with his grandfathers, Lester Flanders, left, and Clarence Vick at the dedication of Camp Vick on July 13, 1958.*

About that same time, classmates of my father had a plaque dedicated to my parents at Colgate Rochester Divinity School. It hung on the wall outside the president's office until the recent sale of the property. When my Vick grandparents and I attended national Baptist events, leaders of the denomination would tell me of the impact my parents had on so many people. These expressions were both a source of pride for me as well as a source of a fear that I could never measure up.

All of this led me on a lifelong journey to find my own identity and my own path. One of my greatest fears was failure. I found myself working harder to achieve "success" at every level. That realization began to emerge in high school when I saw my peers flourishing academically while I was just getting by. It began to dawn on me that I was accountable for what I would accomplish with my life. I needed to break away from what

Paul with his mother, Dorothy. Paul developed a close relationship with her relatives in New York and Michigan.

*Paul Vick with his grandparents
Ethel and Clarence Vick at
Colgate Rochester Divinity
School at the dedication of a
plaque given by Robert Vick's
1943 class memorializing his call
to serve on the mission field.*

I perceived as the expectations of others and create my own expectations for myself. The feeling that I was never "good enough" became a driving force. I felt I had to work longer and harder than the next person to succeed.

I gradually grew an awareness of a feeling of loss. In my early years, that feeling was somewhat muted by a loving family surrounding me. As I grew into greater awareness of self, my understanding of how fragile life could be also became more acute. Grandpa and Grandma Vick, who parented me on a daily basis, were of advancing age. When they were late coming home from work or a meeting, I became anxious that something might have happened to them. They were not physically able to participate in activities in the same way as other parents. I was often left to my own devices. I became increasingly self-reliant, driven by an instinct for self-preservation.

The confluence of these forces can be seen in the life decisions I have made. My early years were lived in an environment grounded in the life that my parents lived. Even when I left for Kalamazoo College, I was never far from my mother's relatives in Michigan. Upon graduation, I moved back to Rochester and attended the same seminary as my father. The seminary president, provost, and some faculty members knew my parents. My first marriage grew out of the church that I, and my father before me, attended. My ecumenical community outreach work took place in the community in which I was raised. After law school, I returned to Rochester and continued my involvement in the life of my church, the American Baptist Region, and the divinity school. In all my travels throughout life, I have always returned to Rochester, the place most closely connected to my family.

While my emotional bond with this community may in some way be tied to my parents and family, the path I have taken and continue on is unique to me. My aptitude, skills, and temperament are significantly different than my parents. I have learned to embrace fully these amazing people who gave me life and how they have helped shape who I have become. But I also have come to understand the unique gifts that God has embedded within me and the opportunities God has presented to me to apply those gifts to serve others. In my heart, I know that my parents continue to be present in my life in a very real way, urging me to stay true to the path God has laid before me.

How this next chapter in my life will unfold, only God knows. I do know that I have been richly blessed, not only by this amazing family into which I was born, but in the gift of children and grandchildren and the joy in seeing them grow into their own persons. As I reflect on the past seventy-five years of my life, I echo the words first uttered by Adoniram Judson, who paved the way for the formation of the American Baptist Foreign Mission Society in 1814: "The future is as bright as God's promises."

Great grandchildren of Robert and Dorothy Vick. FROM LEFT *Aidan Lazenby, Jack Lazenby (at back), Charlie Vick (in carrier), Melinda Lazenby, Grace Vick, Avery Vick, and Emma Vick.*

Appendix

Letter from CNAC pilot Red Holmes
to Paul and Clarence Vick

Amarillo, Texas
January 8th, 1958

Dear Paul and Mr. Vick,

It was nice to locate you people and say hello last Sunday afternoon. I have (been) wondering about you for several years, although you wouldn't remember me, or even recognize my name.

I hadn't anticipated too much difficulty locating you, but it took almost two hours to find the right telephone number. The Rochester Operator could not give us any phone numbers without knowing the initials or the address. I had a scrap book and some clipping from Chinese newspapers which indicated your father's name was Robert, so I started with that, hoping that your grandfather's name might be the same. That phone didn't answer for a long time, and then they did not know you. Next, we ask(ed) the operator for the name of a newspaper there, but since I didn't know the name or address, she could not give me any numbers. The Chinese newspapers mentioned that your parents were Baptist Missionarys, so we called a Baptist Church, and a lady told us the names and phone numbers of two newspapers.

We called the newspaper, the Chronicle, I believe, and they told us to call back in about fifteen minutes. We thought the newspaper

Amarillo, Texas
January 8th, 1958

Dear Paul and Mr. Vick,

It was nice to locate you people and say hello last Sunday afternoon. I have
wondering about you for several years, although, you wouldn't remember me, or
even recognize my name.

I hadn't anticipated too much difficulty locating you, but it took almost two
hours to find the right telephone number. The Rochester Operator could not
give us any phone numbers without knowing the initials or the address. I had
a scrap book and some clippings from Chinese newspapers which indicated your
fathers name was Robert, so I started with that, hoping that your grandfathers
name might be the same. That phone didn't answer for a long time and then they
did not know you. Next, we ask the operator for the name of a newspaper there,
but since I didn't know the name or address, she could not give me any numbers.
The Chinese newspapers mentioned that your parents were Baptist Missionarys, so
we called a Baptist Church, and a lady told us the names and phone numbers of
two newspapers. We called the newspaper, the Chronicle, I believe, and they
told us to call back in about fifteen minutes. We thought the newspaper would
be able to look back thru their files and give Mr. Vick's number. While we were
waiting the fifteen minutes before calling again, one of my small children took
the other phone off the hook. The telephone company finally called with a special
ring to tell us the phone was off the hook. Then we got a man on the City Desk
at the Chronicle, and he had been trying to locate a story about you back in 1947,
but found that both newspapers were on strike about time, so we asked him to give
about ten phone numbers listed under Vick. Several didn't answer, some were busy,
but finally we called a George Vick, I believe, and they knew who you were and
that your Grandfather was named Clarence.

I have been pretty busy since. Yesterday, a friend of mine was buying another
clothing store here in Amarillo. There is an identical store in Odessa, Texas,
and my friend, Stanley Blackburn has a twin-engine Beechcraft Bonanza, so as I
had some small business in Odessa too, I flew down there with him and his Vice-
President. Odessa is about 250 miles due south of Amarillo. We had a tail wind
so it only took us an hour to go, but longer coming back, as we had to stop in
Lubbock while he went into the Bank and closed up the deal.

I was born in Dalhart, Texas, 41 years ago, moved to Amarillo after I finished
high school in 1935. I learned to fly in 1940, went to work as a pilot for
China National Aviation Corporation in 1943. I was released by them in 1948
on account of stomach ulcers and moved back to Amarillo. My wife and I got
married Sept. 5th, 1945 at St Patrick's Cathedral, in New York City, and spent
about 25 days of our honeymoon in New York City. I went back over to China,
leaving New York the night of Sept. 30th, 1945, which was the date of your birth.
Mr. Henry Luce, the editor of Time, Life and Fortune Magazines was also a passenger
on the plane and I became well acquainted with him. In 1954, we organized an
alumni association of CNAC in New York, attending the convention of the Flying
Tigers. I was elected the first president of our organization. We have a reunion
every two years, in 1956 it was held in Miami, Florida, but we were unable to
attend as we were having our fifth baby. Our next convention will be this year
in Los Angeles, Calif.

We have five children, two girls and three boys, Patty is the oldest, she was
born in Shanghai, China, November 12th, 1946. Three boys and the last one a girl,
were all born here in Amarillo. I own a Fast Carwash business here in Amarillo

*The first page of a three-page letter that CNAC pilot Red Holmes sent to Paul
and his grandfather Clarence Vick eleven years after the crash. Holmes details
his journey of flying to West China to retrieve Paul and then ferry him to
Shanghai to recuperate.*

would be able to look thru their files and give Mr. Vick's number. While we were waiting the fifteen minutes before calling again, one of my small children took the other phone off the hook. The telephone company finally called with a special ring to tell us the phone was off the hook. Then we got a man on the City Desk at the Chronicle, and he had been trying to locate a story about you back in 1947 but found that both newspapers were on strike about (that) time, so we asked him to give about ten phone numbers listed under Vick. Several didn't answer, some were busy, but finally we called a George Vick, I believe, and he knew who you were and that your grandfather was named Clarence.

I have been really busy since. Yesterday, a friend of mine was buying another clothing store here in Amarillo. There is an identical store in Odessa, Texas, and my friend, Stanley Blackburn, has a tiny-engine Beechcraft Bonanza, so as I had some small business in Odessa too, I flew down there with him and his Vice-President. Odessa is about 250 miles due south of Amarillo. We had a tail wind so it only took us an hour to go, but longer coming back, as we had to stop in Lubbock while he went into the bank and closed up the deal.

I was born in Dalhart, Texas, 41 years ago, moved to Amarillo after I finished high school in 1935. I learned to fly in 1940, went to work as a pilot for China National Aviation Corporation in 1943. I was released by them in 1948 on account of stomach ulcers and moved back to Amarillo. My wife and I got married Sept. 5th, 1945, at St. Patrick's Cathedral in New York City, and we spent about 25 days of our honeymoon in New York City. I went back over to China, leaving New York the night of Sept. 30th, 1945, which was the date of your birth. Mr. Henry Luce, the Editor of Time, Life and Fortune magazines was also a passenger on the plane and I became well acquainted with him. In 1954, we organized an alumni association of CNAC in New York, attending the convention of the Flying Tigers. I was elected the first president of our organization. We have a reunion every two years; in 1956 it was held in Miami, Florida, but we were unable to attend as we were having our fifth baby. Our next convention will be this year in Los Angeles, Calif.

We have five children, two girls and three boys. Patty is the oldest, she was born in Shanghai, China, Nov. 12th, 1946. Three boys and the last one a girl were all born here in Amarillo. I own a Fast Carwash business here in Amarillo, which I built about six years ago. Business has been pretty good for the past year, since the drought broke. I have a manager who runs it, and I have been devoting some of my time to writing some stories, which I have wanted to do for a long time.

I hope to someday write an article about your experience, and mine in connection with it. I was assistant Chief Pilot when the plane No. 145, on which you were riding, became overdue. We began an immediate search, and the plane was located near the town of Tianmen, about 90 miles west of Hankow, which is 425 miles west of Shanghai. We were informed by radio from Tianmen that there were some survivors. We anticipated that it would take about three (days) to get there by automobile, and there was no airport closer than Hankow. A man, whose name I don't recall, had the distributorship for the little Piper Cubs in Shanghai, but the Chinese Government would not allow it more than fifteen miles from the Shanghai Airport. It was the only aircraft that small in all of China, but it didn't carry enough gas to fly the 425 miles to Hankow.

So we took the wings and tail off, loaded into a big airplane, and I flew it to Hankow, where two mechanics, who had never seen a Piper Cub, put it back together. I test flew it, then they got it back together to make sure it would fly, then loaded our company Doctor, Charles F. Hoey, who was from St. Louis, and has since passed away into the Cub, and we took off for the scene of the crash. All of the land around Tianmen is farmed; they irrigate thru (sic) deep ditches, and the sod fields are very small and at that time were plowed, making the ground real soft. It was difficult to find a field large enough to set even the Cub down.

I first landed near the wreckage of our ill-fated plane, and the big airplane flying over us dropped us a note, telling us to go back about fifteen miles to the town of Tianmen, where the survivors could be found. When we took off, the curious Chinese farmers

lined both sides of our small field solid. As we started taking off,
about a half dozen Chinese started changing sides; we almost hit
one of the last ones; he had to fall flat on the ground to keep the
propeller from striking him. We found the field near the town even
smaller, in fact the largest one close to the walled city was a double
basketball court inside the wall. It was too close to the wall, so we
had to land about one mile away. The plowed ground was so soft
that we only rolled about ten feet after landing. The field, which
I stepped off, was about 150 feet long between ditches about four
feet wide. The doctor started walking into town following a foot
trail and occasionally crossing a sod field.

The big ship overhead began dropping medical supplies near
the Cub, and almost immediately the curious farmers began
gathering around the small Cub. I am enclosing a photograph
taken about twenty minutes after we landed, which will give you
an idea of the crowd; by the time we had been on the ground an
hour, I figure there was 10,000 people in the crowd. To keep the
crowd from getting too close and damaging the Cub, I kept the
engine running, revving it up to blow dirt and dust in their faces;
then getting out, picking up the tail, moving it to another group
and sand blasting them.

Before too long, 200 soldiers broke thru the crowd, set up machine
guns which they fired over the heads of the crowd, and in a further
attempt to keep them back, swung their bayonets at the chins of
the first row. I had the first three or four rows sit down to keep the
crowd from pushing them too close to the Cub, but the pushing
became so strong that they had to stand up to keep from getting
trampled. It was about an hour before anyone showed up who
could speak English, so I was pretty busy with the sign language.
The crowd resented the soldiers and began throwing clods of dirt at
them; they punched several holes in the fabric covering on the Cub.

It began to get dark, when a runner brought a message from
Dr. Hoey, saying that you were the only survivor, and we would
leave at sun-up. I slept with the Cub, after moving it to safer
quarters over near the house at the top of the photo. A heavy frost
fell that night, and you have to scrape it off an airplane before

taking off. About 600 of the Chinese farmers stayed around all night, talking. You see they had never seen an airplane on the ground before. But the 200 soldiers kept good order.

They kept me awake most of the night, talking, bumming cigarettes and matches. The next morning, I put the soldiers to work trampling down the soft field so we could take off better, while I scraped the frost off the wings. We had to leave all our supplies in the custody of the Mayor's son. Dr. Hoey arrived about sun-up with a couple of Chinese carrying you on an improvised stretcher. We decided he would have to hold you on his lap, but in order to have room in the small plane, we had to take out his set of controls, and I had to sit at the other controls, from which you can't see as well. The little ship still had too much frost, but we had to get out of there before the crowd arrived again, and we had a little extra weight, but no wind to shorten our take-off run. Just about everything was not in our favor, even the motor was not up to par. I pulled the Cub tail right up against the ditch, opened the throttle wide open while standing on the brakes, then we started our take-off run. I had just enough speed to jump the next ditch, then we settled back onto the next plowed field; then I saw a mound of dirt covering a grave, which was about four feet high; we managed to jump that (and) settled back on the other side, before we got enough speed to fly. The rest of the trip to Hankow was uneventful.

On the way, Dr. Hoey filled me in on the details he had learned in Tianmen. I believe Farther McCarthy told him your father had jumped out of the burning airplane after it passed over Tianmen about two miles, with you in his arms. They brought you both to a small hospital they had there and your father lived from 40 to 50 hours, telling Father where you were to be sent. I never was clear whether you had one or both legs broken. We don't know what altitude you left the plane but it landed over ten miles from you.

When we arrived at the big airport in Hankow, the mechanics had a small cradle made of aluminum, and lined with blankets, and I flew the plane back to Shanghai. They took you to the Country Hospital, until you recovered sufficiently to be flown back to the United States.

I am going to have to cut this letter short for you, but you will find four photographs; one of you covered with blankets sleeping in the cradle they made for you in the big airplane; two of the plane 145 whose wing burned off and fell about two miles before the plane did; and one of the Cub with the crowd around it about twenty minutes after it landed. I have a few more, and some newspaper clippings, which are glued in the scrap book; maybe I can have them copied or something and send you some.

Now these four pictures are the only copies I have, <u>so be sure to return them, as someone else took the pictures; I do not have the negatives.</u>

<u>If you people could add any information you might have learned from Father McCarthy or any other source, I would greatly appreciate it. Also, be sure to return the snapshots. You might be able to get a photographer to make you a copy if you want.</u>

Best regards,

R.S. (Red) Holmes Jr.
1004 Lamar Street
Amarillo, Texas

Acknowledgments

Where The Cotton Grows is the culmination of a nearly twelve-year journey that took me back through several generations and to several locales.

I traveled from Rochester, New York, to San Francisco, California, from which my family and I had boarded a ship bound for China in late 1946. I attended reunions of pilots who had flown planes for China National Aviation Corporation during the 1940s. I searched through records of the American Baptist Historical Society at Mercer College in Atlanta, Georgia. In 2011, I returned to China for the first time since the plane crash, tracing the path taken by my family and me while in China in 1947. Seeking even more answers, I flew back to China in 2015 to complete the unfinished journey of my parents and brother. I visited Chengdu, where my parents planned to study Chinese dialect, and Yipin, where my parents were to have served as missionaries. In my home in Rochester, I traversed my way through photograph albums and boxes of letters and newspaper and magazine articles that reported on the airplane crash and the impact that singular event had on the lives of so many.

Along the way I have been assisted and encouraged by many. I am indebted to Rev. Dr. Reid Trulson, retired executive director of American Baptist Foreign Mission Society (International Ministries), who first planted the seeds leading to my return to China, and who consented to writing the Foreword to this book. I am also indebted to Rev. Dr. Benjamin S. L. Chan, International Ministry's area director for East and South Asia, in laying the groundwork for my return to China and using his network through the China Christian Council to open doorways to people and places I would not otherwise have been able to access.

I am thankful for the willingness of Rev. David Wong and his wife, Kathy, who accompanied my wife, Joyce, and I on our return trip to China in 2015 and for the expertise of Stanley Chow, who traveled with us on both trips to China, memorializing those trips through the production

175

of the video *The Vineyard*, which is available on YouTube. I am grateful for the willingness of the following for their review of the manuscript and endorsement: Rev. Chan; Dr. Jerry B. Cain, chancellor, Judson University; Rev. Angela Sims, PhD, president of Colgate Rochester Crozer Divinity School; Rev. Reginald Mills, PhD, past president of the board of directors of American Baptist International Ministries; and Rev. Dr. Sandra Hasenauer, executive minister of the American Baptist Churches of Rochester Genesee Region.

I am also thankful for the work of Jane Sutter, for editing this book, and Susan Welt, for the design work necessary to give life to this story through pictures and graphics, and to both of them for guiding me through the steps of publication. Most of all, I want to express heartfelt gratitude to my wife, Joyce, for her ongoing support and encouragement to undertake this project and for traveling with me every step of this journey.

About the Author

Paul A. Vick is an ordained American Baptist Minister and is licensed to practice law in the State of New York. He currently serves as treasurer of the board of the American Baptist Foreign Mission Society (also known as International Ministries) as well as chair of the finance committee of the board of trustees of Colgate Rochester Crozer Divinity School. Paul also serves on the board of the American Baptist Churches of Rochester Genesee Region of the American Baptist Churches USA and is a member of Immanuel Baptist Church in Rochester, New York. He has acted as legal counsel for many civic and religious service organizations. Paul retired as partner in charge of the Family Wealth Planning Department of the Rochester office of Phillips, Lytle LLP in 2007. Paul has made two trips to China. A video called *The Vineyard* documents Paul's most recent trip and can be viewed on YouTube. He is married to Joyce Miller Vick and has three children and seven grandchildren. This is his first book.